SCOTLAND

CHURCH AND NATION THROUGH SIXTEEN CENTURIES

KU-206-303

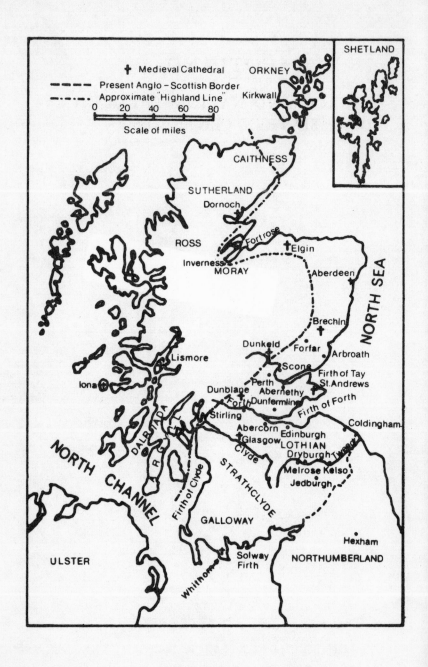

SCOTLAND

CHURCH AND NATION THROUGH SIXTEEN CENTURIES

GORDON DONALDSON
D.Litt.

*Professor of Scottish History
in the University of Edinburgh*

SCOTTISH ACADEMIC PRESS
EDINBURGH & LONDON

FIRST PUBLISHED 1960 BY SCM PRESS LTD

Second Edition published by
Scottish Academic Press Ltd.
25 Perth Street, Edinburgh 3

Distributed by
Chatto and Windus Ltd.
40 William IV Street
London WC2

ISBN 0 7011 1909 8

© 1972 GORDON DONALDSON

All rights reserved. No part of this publication may be repro-
duced, stored in a retrieval system or transmitted, in any
form, or by any means, electronic, mechanical, photocopying,
recording or otherwise, without the prior permission of the
Scottish Academic Press Ltd., 25 Perth Street, Edinburgh 3

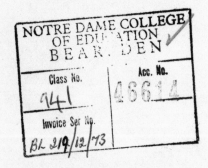

NOTRE DAME COLLEGE
OF EDUCATION
BEARSDEN

Class No.
941

Acc. No.
46614

Invoice Ser No.
BL 219/12/73

Printed in Great Britain by
R. & R. Clark, Ltd., Edinburgh

CONTENTS

I

THE CELTIC PERIOD

CHRISTIANITY in Scotland began nearly sixteen centuries ago, during the last years of the Roman occupation of Britain. Most of the land which afterwards became the kingdom of England had at that time been for three hundred years a settled province of an empire which was in its later years a Christian empire and an instrument for the spread of Christianity as far as its sway extended. The Romans had never subdued the territory north of the Forth and Clyde, and their military occupation of even the south of what is now Scotland had been intermittent, but the native princes who ruled near the frontier of the Roman province had been partially Romanized. It was in the Romano-British civilization of southern Scotland that Scottish Christianity began.

There is good archaeological evidence, mainly in the form of inscribed stones, that Christianity existed in south-west Scotland by the fifth century, and all our knowledge of the period tends to support in outline the tradition recounted by later writers about the work of Ninian, the first missionary to Scotland whose name is known. It is related that Ninian was a native Briton who, after studying at Rome, had been consecrated a bishop, and that about the year 400 he built at Whithorn a church of white stone—his *Candida Casa* or White House. Ninian is credited also with missionary work beyond the sphere of Roman influence, among the 'southern Picts' who probably inhabited the territory roughly between the Firth of Forth and Aberdeen, but how far Ninian and disciples of Ninian planted Christianity in that area and possibly even further north remains a matter of dispute.

During a century and more after Ninian's day, while Christianity certainly continued in south-western Scotland, so far as the rest of the country is concerned there are only faint traces of the missionary work of some very shadowy figures. The developments of this period which were to have most effect on the future of Scotland had their origins overseas: after the departure of the Romans, pagan invaders from the Continent drove the Christian Britons into the western parts of the former Roman province, and among those invaders were the Angles, who crossed the North Sea to occupy north-eastern England and south-eastern Scotland; but Christianity had meantime reached Ireland and Irish invaders called Scots crossed the North Channel from Ulster to form the kingdom of Dalriada in western Scotland, so opening it up to Christian influence from Ireland. The Angles were Teutonic or Germanic in race, but the Irish, like the Britons and Picts, were Celtic, and the Celtic peoples of Scotland, Wales and Ireland had much in common.

Columba, an Irish prince who had studied in monasteries in his own land, settled in Iona in 563. Besides strengthening and extending Christianity among his compatriots, the people of Dalriada, he is credited with the conversion of the 'northern Picts', in the central and northern Highlands. The community which he founded in Iona attained pre-eminence among the early ecclesiastical centres of Scotland, but Columba seems to have been only one missionary among many who were active at this period. By the date of his death (597) the Christian Church had probably been introduced to the greater part of modern Scotland, but it is not clear if Columba himself had been the main agent in the process.

The church, it can at once be observed, is older by several centuries than the nation, for it was only after the year 1000 that anything like the present Scotland emerged, with its frontier on the Tweed.[1] And the church played its part in the making of the nation. Political institutions were then rudimentary, and government a matter of strong kings and chiefs

[1] See p. 16 below.

rather than of administrative machinery. The church, however, was an institution long before the state was, and there are indications that the church made a real contribution to the unification of Scotland and to the making of one kingdom out of those warring Angles, Britons, Picts and Scots who fourteen hundred years ago inhabited the land we now call Scotland. The process was one in which Scotland's relations with her neighbours in the south were closely involved; and at every stage in the process there was recurrent tension between two rival principles—between the narrower, national or regional loyalty and the wider, European or universal loyalty, between indigenous or native influences and foreign or external influences.

The church order which had evolved in Ireland and within which Columba and his successors worked in Scotland was peculiar, partly because it had developed in conformity with the tribal society which it served and partly because the Celtic churches were for a time isolated from the other churches of western Europe. The system was based not on any territorial arrangement but on monasteries, which alone provided priests to minister to the people, and as there were no clergy other than monks there was no place for a diocesan episcopate; jurisdiction over monks pertained, then as always, to the abbot of the monastery, who might be only a presbyter. Bishops were numerous, and although in this situation they might have no jurisdiction they were superior to presbyters in order, they conferred ordination and they had certain privileges in the celebration of Holy Communion. The insignificance of the Celtic bishop's office in an administrative sense was later to encourage the idea that the church in this period was presbyterian and such a myth has a long and not entirely disreputable pedigree. It happened that later Scots, not content with the undoubted fact that their ancestors had received Christianity before the English, were patriotically determined to ante-date the beginning of Scottish Christianity by two or three centuries, and then encountered the difficulty that in 431 Palladius became the 'first bishop of the Scots' (who at that time were still in Ireland); it seemed that the only way to reconcile fact and fiction was to conclude that the people of Scotland were Christians long before they had bishops. At any rate, the priest who wrote the *Scotichronicon* in the fourteenth century said that the first Scottish Christians had 'teachers of the faith and ministers of the sacraments, but only of the rank of presbyters or monks, following the order of the primitive church',[1] and an early sixteenth-century humanist said that the people of Scotland were at first 'instructed in the faith by priests and monks without bishops'.[2] But if it is quite erroneous to regard the Celtic church as presbyterian, it is less inaccurate to describe it as 'independent' or autonomous, for, although there is no reason to believe that it was at variance doctrinally with the rest of western Christendom, it acknowledged no external authority in matters of discipline and rites.

In a church so constituted, tension was almost bound to arise when external influences were encountered, and it first arose less than a century after Columba's time. From his foundation at Iona a mission under Aidan went in 635 to the Anglian kingdom of Northumbria, which stretched from the Forth south to the Humber; but in the year of Columba's death Augustine had landed in Kent, sent by Pope Gregory the Great to bring a mission direct from Rome to the pagan peoples of England. Augustine himself had found that the bishops of the Britons whom he encountered in the south declined to acknowledge the authority of the Pope or to accept himself as their archbishop, and when the Roman mission reached northern England a conflict developed between its usages and those of the Columban churchmen. The matters in question were the seemingly trivial ones of the method of calculating the date of Easter and the manner of tonsuring the heads of the clergy, but there was involved the wider issue of the acceptance or rejection of the authority of the see of Rome over such matters. At the Synod of Whitby, in 663 or 664, Oswiu, king of Northumbria, decided in favour of the Roman

[1] *Scotichronicon*, III, viii.
[2] John Major, *Greater Britain* (Scottish History Society 10, 1892), p. 65.

party and their patron St Peter, the keeper of the keys, and the adherents of the Columban tradition had to retreat northwards. This Roman success in Northumbria was followed up. The Angles were at that time pursuing an aggressive policy against the Picts, and in 685 their army penetrated north of the Tay, to be defeated at Nechtansmere, near Forfar. After this reverse, Northumbria never again tried to subdue the Picts by force of arms, but southern influence, thus worsted in the field, was presently to win a victory in the ecclesiastical sphere, when the Pictish kingdom followed the example of the Angles in rejecting Columba in favour of Peter.

How prolonged and how bitter may have been the controversy within Pictland between the adherents of Peter, representing external influence, and those of Columba, representing native influence, we can only guess. But when Nechtan, king of the Picts, who had put his kingdom under the protection of St Peter (711), expelled from his dominions the Columban clergy who would not accept the Roman uses (717), we have the first known instance of a Scottish government imposing ecclesiastical changes and depriving the clergy who would not accept them. The pattern was to be many times repeated. Certain changes in organization followed the Pictish acceptance of Roman authority: even before the Synod of Whitby, as the Columban church had extended into England, there had been signs of the emergence of something like a territorial episcopate, and after Whitby, first in Northumbria (at Hexham near the present Border and at Abercorn on the Firth of Forth), and then in Pictland (at Abernethy and probably elsewhere), a system of episcopal sees developed. It seemed, early in the eighth century, that throughout eastern and central Scotland the church was going to become indistinguishable from the church in England.

But in the western Irish kingdom of Dalriada, to which the non-conforming clergy had been forced to return, the triumph of the new ways was not complete. The Roman ruling on the date of Easter was indeed accepted, after some debate, even in Iona itself, but the church of Dalriada clearly retained much of its monastic character and such peculiarities in other respects that its ordinations were rejected, and its usages condemned, by councils in England and France. The Pictish kingdom was far more extensive and populous than Dalriada, and the famous sculptured stones which are the chief memorials of the Picts suggest that in organization and efficiency, as well as culture, they were superior to the Scots. Yet in 844, when the lands north of the Forth and Clyde became the united kingdom of Alba, it was the king of the Scots who became king also of the Picts. Irish influence then swept into Pictland, the Scots spread their Gaelic language and, with their conservative tradition, evidently dominated the ecclesiastical life of the united kingdom. The result was something of a reaction which retarded or interrupted the progress of the Pictish church towards assimilation to the normal model, for the united kingdom had to have a united church. It happened that the old headquarters of the church of Dalriada, at Iona, had now been destroyed by Norse attacks, and new headquarters were found at Dunkeld, in the heart of Alba, to which relics of Columba were transferred from Iona. In 865 we read of the death of an abbot of Dunkeld who was also 'first bishop of Fortriu'; as Fortriu was another name for Pictland, and as the term 'first bishop' (*primepscop*) signified that he was the chief bishop, or head bishop, of the kingdom, we must conclude that the bishops of Pictland had been subjected to an abbot-bishop of a great monastery of the Columban type. The date of the bishop's death is only twenty years after the union of the two kingdoms, and it does look as if Dunkeld had been chosen as a new ecclesiastical capital, from which the church could exert a unifying influence on the young kingdom. Thus early, therefore, the church seems to be associated with the making of the nation.

But Dunkeld, often called a gateway to the Highlands, was for the Scottish church the way out. The headship of the church of Alba did not long remain there, but was soon established at St Andrews. The transfer to St Andrews suggests that the eastern coastal plain, with its fertile soil and its seaports, was going to play a larger part in the development of Scotland than either the western seaboard or the mountains of Perthshire. It suggests also that Scotland was going to look to the east and to the south, to the continent and to England. As the emphasis of the nation, the kingdom, shifts, so does the seat of authority in the church.

And the name St Andrews is itself significant. The foundation at Dunkeld had been dedicated to Columba, but with the move to the east coast Columba is displaced, and Andrew becomes the patron saint of the kingdom of Alba. We saw how a king of the Picts had put his kingdom under the patronage of St Peter, and it had not been a big step when one of his successors had adopted St Andrew, Peter's brother, as his patron. The cult of St Andrew very likely reached Pictland by way of Hexham, in the north of England, as one feature of the extension among the Picts of the ecclesiastical institutions of Northumbria, but elaborate legends were invented to explain the association of Andrew with the people of Scotland, who were later to claim proudly that their own ancestors had been converted to Christianity by the apostle in person.

St Andrew was of course the first disciple called by our Lord, and the first thing he had done was to bring his brother Peter to Jesus. If his missionary work was done anywhere it was done in Greece and in the regions around the Black Sea, a fact which gave him an important place in the Russian Church, which shared with Scotland the badge representing the saltire-shaped cross on which he was martyred at Patras, on the Gulf of Corinth. His remains were subsequently taken to Constantinople and, much later, in the thirteenth century, to Amalfi. This was all remote enough from the historical inhabitants of Scotland. But the Scots were later to believe that they were descended from a prince of Greece, and Bede had said that the Picts came from Scythia, the region north of the Black Sea. Besides, the Scots claimed to possess relics of the apostle, including an arm bone which signified his readiness to protect them, and this was explained by a fable relating that St Regulus had removed relics of Andrew from Constantinople and brought them to St Andrews. A companion tale related to a King Angus. Angus, king of the Picts from about 730 to 761, was a great warrior, battling against the Scots of Dalriada, the Angles of Northumbria and the Britons of Strathclyde, and legend relates that in one of his campaigns he had a vision of the cross of St Andrew—a white diagonal cross—against the blue sky. King Angus may very well have been the founder of the monastery dedicated to St Andrew which was established at the place in Fife since known by the saint's name. The saltire became the Scottish national emblem and when, much later, it was adopted as the foundation for the Union Jack, the background continued to represent the blue sky against which King Angus saw the white cross twelve hundred years ago.

In the contrast between Columba, the local saint, and Andrew, the apostle of the universal Church, there is again to be seen the tension between native and external influences. And the fact that it was Andrew and not Columba who became the patron saint of Alba, and later of Scotland, indicates that the country had for the time being turned its back on isolation. Just as in Pictland in the eighth century, so now in Alba in the tenth century, it seemed that the church was likely to approximate to other churches. But again there was an obstacle. This time the process of assimilation into the main stream of European development was interrupted by the incursions of the pagan Norsemen. They colonized the north and west of Scotland, they had settlements in the Solway area, they were active along the east coast and they were established in strength in the North of England. This extensive penetration went far to isolate Scotland for a time from the rest of Christian Europe.

During this period of comparative isolation, native influences evidently prevailed in the Scottish Church, which therefore retained certain peculiarities, There is no reason to believe that it held doctrines in any way different from those of the rest of western Christendom, and its substantial agreement with other churches is perhaps sufficiently indicated by the fact that one of the eleventh century-kings—Macbeth[1]—went on a pilgrimage to Rome. Of its organization it is impossible to write with much assurance, owing to the dearth of information. Bishoprics of a territorial or semi-territorial kind may have continued in certain areas from the eighth century, and a territorial organization with a secular or non-monastic clergy must have been developing in some parts of the country. Elsewhere there were still some monasteries of the old 'Columban' type, but there is reason to believe that the office of abbot had become secularized and hereditary, with the result that the bishop would become more important as the principal spiritual officer of the community and would begin to exercise jurisdiction over the house itself and over the local churches attached to it. But Scotland had missed certain developments which had brought about great changes in other countries. On the continent there had been the reforms associated with the monastery of Cluny (founded in 910) and in England Archbishop Dunstan (959–88) had reformed and revived monasticism and suppressed communities of secular priests. In Scotland, by contrast, the monasteries presumably remained unreformed and the most vital bodies in the church were communities of Culdees, who, whatever their origin, were by this time corporations of priests, centred at an important foundation but having local churches attached to them. Clearly over the whole field of organization there was much to be done by way if not of reform at least of integration and systematization. It will become equally clear from what follows that in certain matters of ritual and discipline Scottish practice was not in conformity with that of England and continental countries.

[1] See p. 17 below.

2

RECONSTRUCTION UNDER
QUEEN MARGARET AND HER SONS

WHEN Scottish isolation came to an end, in the eleventh century, the battle between native and external influences had to be fought over again. It is this recurrent tension which lies behind the picturesque story of Duncan and Macbeth, familiar from Shakespeare's play. King Duncan (1034–40) was the first king to rule over a united realm extending much further south than the old kingdom of Alba. The land between the Forth and the Tweed had been ceded to the Scots about 1018, and Duncan had at the same time inherited the British kingdom of Strathclyde, so that when he became king of Scots his western frontier extended to the Solway and beyond it. It is now possible to speak of a kingdom of 'Scotland', but Duncan's dominions were far from homogeneous. The lands south of the Forth and Clyde contained elements alien to the kingdom of Alba, and the inclusion of Lothian meant that Scotland now contained an Anglian or English element which was to play a part in the future development of the country far out of proportion to its size. From Duncan's reign onwards, Scotland was no longer a purely Celtic country, and in all the centuries that have passed since his reign the importance of the Celtic element, linguistically and culturally, has steadily diminished. Here, within Scotland itself, was a source of tension, which had its bearing on the development of church and state alike.

Duncan was the son of a daughter of Malcolm II by Crinan, Abbot of Dunkeld, and his grandfather had nominated him as his heir, although the custom in Alba had been that the eldest, or ablest, male of the royal house, rather than the direct heir by primogeniture, should succeed. Duncan, besides, married a Northumbrian lady and was thus the first of many kings to introduce such a southern influence to the Scottish court. On the other hand, both Macbeth and his wife belonged to the Alban royal family and had a good claim to the throne according to the old rules of inheritance. Macbeth's action in defeating Duncan in battle and slaying him may thus have represented a native or Celtic reaction against the anglophile Duncan. During the seventeen years of Macbeth's reign, Duncan's son Malcolm took refuge in England, and it was with southern help that he ultimately overthrew Macbeth and gained his father's throne. There were already, therefore, pro-English elements in the Scottish kingdom before King Malcolm married the English princess Margaret, about the year 1070.

Margaret belonged to the old English royal family which had been excluded from the throne first by Canute and the other Danish kings and again (after the reign of her great-uncle, Edward the Confessor) by William the Conqueror. She was probably born in Hungary, where she spent her early years as an exile, and after the Norman Conquest of England, again a refugee, she was received in Scotland by Malcolm. Not only was she familiar with English usage and organization, but she had a zeal which may have owed something to her experience of Hungary, a country which had been converted to Christianity only a generation or two earlier.

With such a background, it was inevitable that Margaret should endeavour to prevail on the Scottish clergy to lay aside practices which she considered to be old-fashioned, if not lax. She demanded that Lent should begin on Ash Wednesday and not on the following Monday, and she procured the condemnation of marriage with a step-mother or with a brother's widow. She argued against the reluctance of the Scots to receive Communion, arising as it did from a sense of unworthiness which she considered exaggerated—a feature

B

of Celtic church life which has been persistent, for to this day some of the most pious Highlanders are most unwilling to communicate. She sought to eradicate the custom of celebrating mass with a 'barbarous rite, contrary to the custom of the whole Church', which has been taken to suggest that the Scots were using Gaelic. And she introduced the rigours of the Scottish Sabbath by insisting that Sunday should be not only a day of abstinence from labour but a day when 'we apply ourselves only to prayers'.

Such were the Five Articles of Queen Margaret, which may have been as divisive in their effect on the Scottish church as the Five Articles of Perth[1] were to be five hundred years later. The interviews with the native clergy in which the queen pressed her innovations are known to us only from a narrative by her admiring confessor, and her opponents have not left on record what they thought about it all. One can only guess that King Malcolm's strong arm had a good deal to do with her success and that the development therefore falls into the recurrent pattern of the imposition of ecclesiastical changes by the crown. Margaret was in any event no religious recluse, but, it has been said, 'one of those strong, interfering, pious and persistent women of whom England has bred a considerable number'. While the political side of her activities is largely concealed from us, we do know that she did not stop her husband from undertaking a series of devastating invasions of the north of England, with a view to harassing the Norman kings who had dispossessed her family. That there was opposition to the Anglicizing policy of Malcolm and Margaret emerged as soon as they were removed from the scene, for their deaths (1093) were immediately followed by a Celtic or native reaction which for a time excluded their sons from the throne.

Margaret's programme had at the best been a limited one. So far from trying to subvert the existing ecclesiastical organization, she gave additional endowments to the Culdees and one of her own sons became abbot of the ancient mona-

[1] See p. 81 below.

stery of Dunkeld, and she did nothing, apart from bringing a few Benedictine monks to Dunfermline, to foster and endow new institutions. How far the limited changes which she made would in themselves have been effective in making the Scottish church identical with those of England and other countries it is hard to say. The achievement of Margaret which was most influential on the Scottish church and the Scottish nation was the achievement, uncommon in saints, of producing six sons and two daughters.

down-plays her role

Three of her sons reigned in succession as Edgar, Alexander I and David I. They did not gain their throne unopposed, for they had first to overcome the native reaction against southern nfluence which had followed the deaths of their parents, and they were able to do so only with military aid from England. Sons of an English mother, refugees in England on their parents' deaths, set on the Scottish throne with English assistance, and the first of them little more than a client of the English king, they maintained the closest relations with England. Their sister married Henry I of England, so that, when Alexander I was on the throne (1107–24), David was at once brother of the king of Scots and brother of the queen of England, and as the owner of wide estates in England he was the first subject of that kingdom before he succeeded to the Scottish throne. To all intents and purposes an Anglo-Norman noble, he had been, as an English chronicler remarked in his patronizing way, 'polished from his boyhood by his intercourse and friendship with us'. The chronicler was evidently of the same mind as Dr Johnson, who remarked that much may be made of a Scotsman if he be caught young. The reigns of those sons of Margaret saw a Norman Conquest of Scotland, partly indeed by war, in the sense that it was southern intervention which established the dynasty on the Scottish throne, but mainly by peaceful penetration.

From Norman England there came Englishmen, Anglo-Normans and members of families which had originated in various parts of northern France, to become landowners in

Scotland and to fill the highest positions in state and church. It was French families which were to give Scotland her future kings—Balliols, Bruces and Stewarts—and familiar Scottish surnames like Cuming, Fraser, Graham, Hay, Melville, Moubray, Ramsay and Somerville made their first appearance with this twelfth-century influx from the south. Scotland was progressively brought into line with Norman England in government, in social structure and in culture, and the old native institutions, based on tribal or clan relationships and on kinship, were largely superseded. The realm was organized, as never before, on the basis of the feudal method of land-holding and on a system of administration under royal officials operating in the king's court at the centre and the king's castles in the localities. The object of government policy was the formation of a Scottish state, the development of administrative and judicial machinery and the consolidation of the diverse races of Scotland into one people under a dynasty whose rule should be unquestioned.

In the fulfilment of such a policy, ecclesiastical institutions were hardly less important than civil institutions, and the church, as well as the state, was transformed by the sons of Margaret as one aspect of the Norman Conquest. It is in the twelfth century, and not in Margaret's own day, that we first hear of changes which gave the organization of the church a character which it has never since quite lost. Parish churches, each with its clearly defined district, were set up, and were served not by monks subject to an abbot but mainly by resident secular clergy. Now that secular clergy were predominant it was necessary to develop a complete system of territorial dioceses, and by the middle of the twelfth century every Scottish diocese had taken shape except Argyll, which appeared about 1200. Under the bishops appeared archdeacons and rural deans to exercise the oversight of the parish clergy. The territorial organization of the church is to be viewed in relation to the parallel royal policy of developing sheriffdoms, and as bishops had often been royal officials before their appointment they represented the extension of crown authority, while within the diocese the interdependence of the bishop, his subordinates and the local churches represented a regional cohesion which was hardly equalled in civil administration in that period. Ecclesiastical organization, with precedents in the well-established systems of other countries, accompanied political organization, and the uniformity of the ecclesiastical system must have contributed directly to the consolidation and unification of the nation.

But apart from the territorial organization of the secular clergy and the bishoprics, which contained many features novel to Scotland, there was also a great development of monasticism. Monks of the orders which were by this time fashionable on the continent and in England were introduced, and their monasteries lavishly endowed by the king and the nobles. All was in accord with the ideas and practices current throughout the west at the time. Much of the borrowing was from England, but in establishing houses of the Benedictine reform of Tiron, in Brittany, King David introduced to Scotland a rule all but unknown in England, and for other houses he brought monks from Arrouaise and Beauvais. In the following century, again, there were Scottish houses of the Valliscaulian order, which was not represented in England. Scottish isolation had never been so completely broken down.

David was reproached by one of his successors as 'a sair sanct for the croun', who had diverted to the endowment of religion resources which could have been retained for the strengthening of the monarchy, but he knew well that the dividends which his investments would pay were not only spiritual. It is true that the abbeys were founded primarily as centres of devotion, where the monks would keep up their regular round of praise and prayers, and that the great abbey churches which skilled craftsmen were employed to erect and adorn were built primarily not for the accommodation of congregations (though their naves often served as parish churches) but to the glory of God. But the abbeys with their ordered life were always focal points of stability in times of trouble, and some of them did much for the utilization of the economic resources of the country. Each of the several orders of monks had its characteristic contribution to make to the life of the nation. The Cistercians, with their interest in manual labour and skilled crafts as well as in meditation and prayer, did a great deal to develop agriculture; their house at Melrose engaged in sheep-farming on a large scale, and their house at Newbattle pioneered Scottish coal-mining. The Augustinians, or Black Canons, were not confined to the cloister like monks, and undertook the conduct of services in parish churches as well as in their abbey churches, but they also had a reputation for hospitality and for that reason were settled by the kings at sites which were convenient for royal residence—Scone, Holyrood and Cambuskenneth—thereby saving the expense of maintaining palaces. The Premonstratensians, or White Canons, were also canons regular, like the Augustinians, but they followed the example of the Cistercian monks in attaching importance to manual labour. The best known of their houses is Dryburgh. Most of the abbeys, at least in their earlier days, made provision for the relief of the poor, and, although they did not normally conduct schools for outsiders, they were themselves centres where a love of learning was sometimes instilled and maintained. Even in the later and degenerate days of Scottish monasticism, nearly every monk received an education which at least taught him to sign his name, when this was no common accomplishment. (The same is not true, it should be added, of the nuns, who were mostly illiterate.) It is beyond question that the monasteries were one of the great civilizing influences of the period.

How much opposition the policy of the sons of Margaret encountered in the church does not appear. Facile talk about 'the Roman church' and 'the Celtic church', as if they were two rival denominations existing alongside each other in twelfth-century Scotland and competing for the allegiance of the people, is misleading. It is true that there was a period of perhaps half a century when the structure of ecclesiastical organization was only gradually achieving something like uniformity, and there must have been for a time some variation in rites and discipline: but then, and for many centuries afterwards, there was only one 'church' in Scotland, and no one conceived it possible that there should be more than one. At the same time, it is unlikely that conformity was achieved without the use of some force, and in this respect again a familiar pattern was followed. Certainly the kings had the means and the will to use compulsion, for David put before the Culdees of Loch Leven the alternatives of acceptance of the rule of the Augustinian canons regular or expulsion from their island. Periodical revolts, mainly in the north, showed that there was political opposition to the Anglicizing kings, if only on dynastic and racial grounds. Yet the main evidence of the underlying tension between native and external influences in this period is to be found in the divergent courses taken by secular and ecclesiastical developments. While the general picture of Scottish life and institutions is one of assimilation to England, the church was associated with the maintenance of Scottish independence against external aggression.

3

THE STRUGGLE FOR INDEPENDENCE

EVEN after the reconstruction of the twelfth century there was still one respect in which the organization of the church in Scotland was unlike that of most churches. Throughout western Europe generally, the church was organized also in units larger than dioceses—provinces, each under an archbishop or metropolitan—and it was now the rule that the election of bishops must be confirmed by an archbishop holding authority from the Pope. The Scottish church had had its 'chief bishop' or 'head bishop', at Dunkeld in the ninth century and at St Andrews in the tenth and eleventh centuries, but when diocesan organization was completed in the twelfth century no archbishop was set up. Therefore, when the question arose as to who should confirm the election of Scottish bishops, claims came from England that as Scotland had no archbishop it was not a separate province, and it was alleged that one of the English archbishops—Canterbury or York—was the metropolitan of Scotland. Submission might have seemed inevitable, for the sons of Margaret owed their throne to English support and many of the bishops and other leading churchmen had come from south of the Border. But neither the Scottish kings nor the Scottish churchmen would yield to the English claims. The repeated demands of York in particular, and the orders of the Pope that the Scots should give obedience to an English archbishop, were all in vain. As a propaganda measure, the Scots fostered the cult of St Andrew, as their patron: St Andrew of Scotland was a useful counterpoise to St Peter of York; and when it was desirable to impress the

Pope it was useful to recall that he was also the brother of St Peter of Rome.

Even after the Scottish king, William the Lion (1165–1214), was unlucky enough to be captured during an invasion of England and had to acknowledge Henry II of England as his feudal superior, the Scottish bishops would not give way. Summoned to a council at Northampton in 1176 and ordered by the king of England to make submission to the English church, they answered that their predecessors had never been subject to the English church and neither would they be so subject. 'To this replied Roger, Archbishop of York, that the bishops of Scotland had made subjection to the metropolitan church of York in the time of their predecessors . . . and in support of this showed sealed documents which he had at hand. Then a great dispute arose between Roger, Archbishop of York, and Richard, Archbishop of Canterbury, about the receiving of that subjection. For the Archbishop of Canterbury said that the subjection ought to be made to the church of Canterbury, and the Archbishop of York said, to his church. And thus ended that conference.' The Scottish bishops took advantage of the rivalry of York and Canterbury to escape without committing themselves. In the same year, 1176, the Pope gave way to the extent of telling the Scots that they were not to obey York unless York could prove its case. The feudal subjection of the Scottish crown to England came to an end in 1189, and the long disagreement over the ecclesiastical position was cleared up three years later, when the Scottish church was pronounced to be a 'special daughter' of the Roman see, subject only to the Pope himself and to no archbishop. Never since then has any English archbishop had jurisdiction over Scottish bishops.

The supreme organ of church government within Scotland was a provincial council or synod, consisting of the bishops and a selected number of other clergy. It was presided over by one of the bishops, styled 'Conservator of the privileges of the Scottish church' and elected by the synod

at each meeting, an arrangement which ensured that no
bishop should have permanent superiority over his brethren.
Archbishops were set up in Scotland only very much later,
at St Andrews in 1472 and at Glasgow in 1492, and they
lasted for only two hundred years.[1] (The bishoprics of Galloway, Orkney and the Isles were not, in earlier times, part
of the Scottish province. Galloway was subject to York,
and Orkney and the Isles to the Norwegian archbishopric
of Nidaros, now Trondheim. They were formally incorporated in the Scottish province only in 1472.)

It was of great importance that the Scottish battle for independence from England had been fought and won in the
ecclesiastical sphere before the long struggle for political independence began. When Edward I of England attempted
the conquest of Scotland, from 1296 onwards, the secular
magnates, many of whom were of Norman descent and had
estates on both sides of the Border, at first tended either to
support the invader or to be irresolute. But in the struggle
for independence which was led first, unsuccessfully, by
William Wallace and then, successfully, by Robert the Bruce,
churchmen were prominent on the patriotic side, even although the national cause meant hostility not only to England but also to the Pope. At one stage an appeal by the Scots
succeeded in gaining them the Pope's protection, but it was
soon withdrawn, and English arms, instead, received the
papal blessing. To make the position of Scottish churchmen
doubly difficult, Robert the Bruce started his career as leader
of the resistance movement by murdering one of his dynastic
rivals, and murdering him in a church. Yet the kingship of
even a sacrilegious murderer, claiming the throne of a
country largely in enemy occupation, won the support of
patriotic Scottish bishops. Three of them were present when
Bruce was hastily crowned in 1306, and the Bishop of Glasgow, who had given Bruce absolution for his crime of mur-
der, provided from his own sacristy the robes for the king
to wear, as well as bringing forth from concealment the

[1] See p. 107 below.

banner of a former king of Scots. Imprisonment by the English did not shake the resolution of the Scottish prelates, and in 1310, when Bruce had done little more than take the first steps on the path to victory, some of them issued a manifesto justifying their choice of a king and solemnly declaring their determination to adhere to him: 'By the providence of the Supreme King, under whose government kings rule and princes bear sway, we have with divine sanction agreed upon the said Lord Robert, and with the concurrence and consent of the people he was chosen to be king; and with him the faithful people of the kingdom will live and die as with one who is worthy of the name of king and the honour of the kingdom, since, by the grace of the Saviour, he has by the sword restored the realm thus deformed and ruined.' It is only right to add that after Bruce's great victory at Bannockburn (1314), Scottish bishops had a chance to recoup themselves for vestments they had sacrificed at his coronation, because new ones were made out of cloth of gold captured among the spoils of the English camp, to remain among the treasures of the Scottish church until the Reformation, when they were dispersed—not, however, by John Knox or any other reformer, but by that supposedly pious lady, Mary, Queen of Scots, who gave some of them away to her paramour the Earl of Bothwell.[1]

But if Bannockburn brought material compensation and the effective ejection of the English from Scotland, it did not induce a change in the papal attitude. Bruce was not yet recognized as king, the Scottish bishops who supported him (and who declined to appear before the Pope to answer for their action) were excommunicated. At length, in 1320, there went to the Pope a letter which is regarded as the Scottish declaration of independence—a letter indeed of the barons, but composed by the Abbot of Arbroath and undoubtedly approved by the Scottish clergy. The Scots' version of their early history, now in its finished shape, was presented for papal consideration. The kingdom of the Scots, it was said,

[1] D. Hay Fleming, *Mary, Queen of Scots*, 1897, p. 309.

had been ruled by a line of independent kings, one hundred and thirteen in number, all of native stock, without interference from abroad until the advent of the tyrannical Edward. So precious to God had the people of Scotland been that 'our Lord Jesus Christ called these very men, dwelling at the limit of the world, almost the first to his most holy faith, nor would have them confirmed therein through any but the first of his apostles to be called (albeit in rank second or third), namely Andrew the meek, brother of the Blessed Peter, whom he chose to be evermore their leader and patron.' The barons went on to record the services rendered to this chosen people by King Robert, who had been like a Joshua or a Maccabeus, but declared that should he show signs of abandoning the task they would take another for king: 'So long as a hundred of us remain alive we will never be subject to the English king; for it is not for riches, or honours, or glory that we fight, but for liberty alone, which no worthy man loses save with his life.' It was made clear that there was no hope that the war would end by surrender on the part of the Scots, and the letter concluded by telling the Pope that if he would not alter his attitude his soul would be burdened with responsibility for the death and destruction which would ensue.

The Pope was suitably impressed. Almost at once he wrote to the king of England along the lines suggested by the Scots, and in due course the ban on Bruce was removed. Papal permission for his anointing, however, arrived only to find the liberator king dead (1329), and his less worthy son, David II, was the first Scottish king to be anointed. Requests in the previous century for papal permission for the anointing of Scottish kings had always been blocked by the English kings, and Scottish monarchy had thus lacked the ultimate sanction of anointing. Now, however, there was no doubt that Scottish kings were fully sovereign. And at this date, with the bull permitting the anointing of the Scottish kings, we have reached the culminating point in the development of an independent church and an independent nation, the outcome of a long struggle in which the church no less than the nation played its part.

The war with England was to be resumed many times, and in all was to continue intermittently for almost three centuries (1296–1560). But Scotland maintained her independence against all the resources of her mighty southern neighbour, and in the course of this medieval struggle the nationhood of Scotland was made and preserved. The Scots naturally established a military alliance and close cultural relations with England's other enemy, France, and this connection, combined with hostility to England, gave many Scottish institutions, like Scots law and the Scottish university system, a more continental and less insular character than those of England.

The clash with the papacy in the time of Robert the Bruce was not the Scots' only experience of a situation in which they found their national aspirations opposed by the Pope. Two hundred years later, the king of Scots was James IV (1488–1513). In the hope of bringing the war with England to an end, he married a daughter of Henry VII and made with England a 'Treaty of Perpetual Peace' (1502–3). The ultimate result of this marriage was the union of the crowns, one hundred years later, when the great-grandson of James and Margaret succeeded to the English throne; but the immediate results were less happy. James was eager for peace among the kings of Christendom, partly indeed because he could reconcile Scotland's traditional French alliance with his new English alliance only as long as France and England did not go to war, but partly because he wanted to see a united Christian crusade against the Turks, who were by this time threatening central Europe. James's contemporaries did not share his romantic ideals, and one of the hard realists was Pope Julius II, primarily a politician and a soldier. The Pope did form a 'Holy League', which the king of England joined, but it was directed not against the Turks but against the Most Christian King of France, the ancient ally of the Scots. Yet, although this league was purely political, Pope Julius thought that he could use his spiritual powers as supreme pontiff to further his secular aims and keep the Scots neutral when England invaded France. It has been said that the behaviour of the Pope at this juncture was like that of a referee at a football match who dons a jersey and plays for one of the sides, but retains his whistle and insists on declaring his opponents offside whenever they become at all dangerous. King James, despite the fact that he knew he would incur ecclesiastical penalties if he contravened the Treaty of Perpetual Peace, defied the Pope and, supported by bishops and abbots as Bruce had been, invaded England, where he met his death at Flodden (1513). On this occasion, when the Scottish king died excommunicate and when papal policy had contributed to a major disaster to Scottish arms, the Scots may have felt a sharper grievance than they had in Bruce's time, when they had been victorious in spite of the Pope.

How far the fact that the Scots found the papacy on the opposite side in war and diplomacy may itself have influenced their attitude to the Pope's ecclesiastical authority it is hard to say. However, there is ample evidence that the administrative powers of the papacy too were frequently challenged. Papal authority first became a factor in Scottish ecclesiastical administration in the twelfth century, and in the absence of a metropolitan, who in other provinces stood between the bishops and the Pope, each bishopric of the Scottish province stood in a direct relationship with Rome. This meant, for one thing, that the Pope, who had the right to confirm the elections of Scottish bishops, had a judicial power of deciding in disputed appointments, and this brought him into conflict with the Scottish crown as early as the reign of William the Lion. It meant further that appeal lay from the law courts of the Scottish bishops to the Roman court, and the Pope also frequently appointed commissioners to decide on law suits arising in Scotland. At first, the extension of the power of the papacy had been undeniably beneficial. Quite apart from the general supervision which Rome could exercise over the various provinces of the church, and its influence in preserving a broad conformity, the external, international power of the Pope was sometimes a refuge from the pressure of kings or other laymen. Appointments to benefices, including bishoprics, if made locally, might concede too much to the influence of the secular power, and when the Popes took appointments into their own hands it might come about that men who lacked influence with lay patrons could be promoted on their merits.

But as the papal lawyers drew more and more cases to Rome, and as the papal control over appointments in the church was extended from the bishoprics to many other classes of benefices there were recurrent protests against the increasing centralization. Action was taken by the Scottish crown, partly because the kings argued that they must have a voice in the appointment of the bishops and abbots, who would be members of their parliaments and councils, but partly also because the excursions to Rome of ambitious clerics in search of lucrative appointments, and of determined litigants in search of favourable decisions, drained money from the realm. From the reign of James I (1406–37), Scottish parliaments passed successive acts designed to restrain clerical transactions at Rome, to forbid the export of Scottish money, and to retain at home the right to make appointments in the church.

It must not be thought that opposition to the papacy, either in international politics or in administration, involved any disposition to disown the papacy in theory, and the pontiff was always 'our haly fader the Pape'. It might perhaps be said that there was no objection to the papal supremacy as long as it was not too effective. The Scottish church was drawn more closely into association with the western church as a whole in this period than in any other; doctrine, government and worship, though not quite uniform, were much the same everywhere, and the unity of the Christian commonwealth overrode national and provincial boundaries. Yet, however far papal pretensions went, the sense of the identity of the national church was never lost. The church in Scotland, the Scottish province of the church, remained *Ecclesia Scoticana*, the Scottish church: we even find the phrase 'the universal church of Scotland' which was afterwards adopted by the reformers. Scotland was in no sense peculiar in this respect, and she was certainly more closely linked with Rome than England was. But all provinces had a certain autonomy in their internal affairs, and it is not in Scotland alone that there is evidence of continuing tension between independence and submission to an external authority. Scotland did, however, show a somewhat unusual degree of independence during the Great Schism (1378–1417), when there were two—and for a time three—rival Popes to choose from. While England supported the Pope at Rome, Scotland joined her ally France in supporting the Pope at Avignon; but in later years, after all other countries had abandoned the cause of Benedict XIII, Scotland alone continued to adhere to him and so for a time had a Pope of her own. And one wonders whether there are parallels in other countries to that curious episode early in the sixteenth century when a decision that the Scottish church should adopt revised service-books which had been compiled by the bishop of Aberdeen was made not by the Pope or by a church council, but by the Scottish king and his advisers.

Such important truths about Scottish relations with the Pope are apt to be concealed by the habit of referring to the medieval church as 'the Roman Catholic Church' and to the Middle Ages as 'Roman Catholic times'. The trouble has been that many writers of ultra-Protestant views have chosen to identify the church which the reformers condemned with the church to which they themselves were strongly hostile, and have not cared to admit that the Roman Catholic Church has undergone change and reform since the sixteenth century. This customary terminology has obscured the not inconsiderable differences in organization, ceremonial and even doctrine between the medieval church and the Roman Catholic Church of today. It is rare, for example, to find the

sacrificial character of the Eucharist defined in the Middle
Ages in terms which would not be acceptable to, say, a moderate Anglican of the twentieth century; and indeed the timid
statements of a catechism of 1552, that 'The sacrifice of the
altar' is no more than 'ane quick and special remembrance
of the passioun of Christ' or 'ane quick memorial, ordanit
to reduce to our mynd the passioun of Christ',[1] would
hardly be acceptable even to Presbyterians, in whose *Church
Hymnary* appear the lines:

> 'And having with us Him that pleads above,
>   We here present, we here spread forth to Thee
> That only offering perfect in Thine eyes,
> The one true, pure, immortal sacrifice.'

Again, while there was of course no doubt about an objective Real Presence, the reserved Sacrament received something less than the adoration it receives today. It was kept
not in a tabernacle on the altar, but in earlier times presumably in a hanging pyx and in later times usually in a
sacrament-house in the wall of the sanctuary—practices now
generally forbidden in the Roman Communion. While the
monstrance, in which the Sacrament could be shown to the
people, was coming into use, the service of Benediction had
not been introduced. Reverence was paid to the reserved
Sacrament, but genuflexion was expressly forbidden by
Bishop Elphinstone when he made his regulations for his
college at Aberdeen at the end of the fifteenth century. While
the central position of the mass in worship was undisputed,
the emphasis on it was not exclusive, for mattins also was
obligatory for the laity, and the clergy were ordered to say
that service at times convenient for the people. The mass
itself was to be said clearly, and not muttered inaudibly.
While masses were multiplied, and the people were sup-
posed to hear one every Sunday and holy-day, communion

[1] *The catechism of John Hamilton*, ed. Thomas Graves Law, 1884, pp. 203,
205.

C

was very infrequent and the invariable practice was to communicate only once a year, at Easter.

The Ave Maria of our pre-Reformation forefathers consisted only of the scriptural salutation, 'Hail Mary, full of grace, the Lord is with thee, blessed art thou among women and blessed is the Fruit of thy womb, Jesus,' and did not include the petition, 'Holy Mary, Mother of God, pray for us sinners now and at the hour of our death.' The clergy, whether secular or regular, did not then use the style 'Father' as a title, but were usually known as 'Master' or 'Sir', according to whether they had or had not taken a Master's degree at a university. The title 'Sir', applied to a priest, sometimes ignorantly taken to have been a mark of distinction, in fact marked the lack of any distinction whatever. Nor did parish priests then wear the biretta while taking part in a service; indeed, one of the last statutes of a Scottish provincial council expressly forbade the clergy to wear their caps in church, and especially in the choir. The gradine or shelf behind the altar to support candles had not made its appearance; altars rarely had any ornament save a cross and two candlesticks. Some Anglican churches used consciously to model their worship on medieval example, but quite apart from those familiar with such usage, there are many modern churchmen, Anglican and Presbyterian alike, who would find little that is strange in the design and equipment of a medieval church.

When the whole field of government, worship and doctrine is surveyed, what does emerge is that many of the features of modern Roman Catholic life which arouse most emotion among Protestants did not then exist. The issue between the sixteenth-century reformers and the church which they attacked must be thought of along somewhat different lines. Important doctrinal differences there certainly were, for the reformers considered that the church laid too much stress on works, too little on faith; they repudiated as idolatry the adoration of the consecrated elements in the mass; they condemned some notions of the Eucharistic

sacrifice which were popularly held, if not officially coun-
tenanced, as derogating from the redemptive work of Christ;
and they were repelled by the multiplication of private
masses, offered mainly for the release of souls from purgatory.
But the Scottish Reformation was less a movement for a new
theology than one for the reform of life and morals, for the
overhaul of ecclesiastical organization.

4

A CHURCH IN NEED OF REFORM

THE first phase in the period between Queen Margaret and the Reformation had been that of the monasteries, whose work was mentioned in the second chapter. Nearly all the Scottish monasteries were founded within a relatively short period, within the hundred years from about 1120 to 1220, so that by the sixteenth century they were aged and devitalized. The abbot was now seldom more than an administrator of the estates and financial interests of the house, and too often he was a lay 'commendator' who drew the revenues but could be only a titular head of a religious community. The monks, on their side, were living in comfort, each on his individual portion, which was now, for all practical purposes, a salary. There is a stream of testimony, from the late fourteenth century onwards, to the damaged or decaying state of Scottish monastic buildings, and it seems probable that many, perhaps most, of the Scottish abbeys were partially in ruins before 1560. But, while there is thus evidence of a departure from old ideals, and indeed from the rule which monks were pledged to observe, and evidence too of material decay, it would be quite wrong to generalize about what life in a Scottish monastery was like on the eve of the Reformation. The one house with an outstandingly good reputation was the Charterhouse at Perth, Scotland's only house of the strict Carthusian order, whose proud boast it was that it never required to be reformed because it was never deformed, and the Charterhouse was also by far the youngest of Scottish monasteries (1429). At the other extreme were houses whose records look definitely bad. In this category fall all the nunneries except the new foundation at Sciennes, Edinburgh

(1517), probably all the smaller houses for men and also Iona, where in the 1420s there was a nun who was the daughter of one of the monks, suggesting that in those days the Iona community was a close-knit affair. It is not clear if things were much better at Inchcolm, sometimes called the Iona of the east, because there, it is related in the 1420s, the monks had been keeping a woman on the premises for thirteen years.

The great majority of the houses were indifferent, rather than positively good or positively bad. There is little real proof that the monks in general were other than respectable in character, nor are there sweeping allegations against their morals either in the writings of the reformers or in the satirical and sometimes scurrilous rhymes which circulated at the time. For example, the author of notorious verses beginning:

> 'The Paip, that pagane full of pryde,
> He hes us blindit lang',

while he castigates the secular clergy for sexual immorality, makes no such accusations against the monks. The abbot, indeed, he classes with the bishop, who

> 'wald nocht wed ane wyfe,
> Thinkand it was ane lustie lyfe
> Ilk day to have ane new ane,'

but of the rank and file of the monks he has nothing worse to say than that they

> 'Maid gude kail[1] on Frydayis quhen thay fastit,'

which seems a venial enough offence; and, incidentally, the distinction which he makes seems to be corroborated by the records of legitimations, in which, while the children of abbots and priors abound, it is hard to find references to the offspring of monks. 'Respectable but dull' might not unfairly describe the majority of the monasteries. Possibly the most damning fact is that when the Reformation came the cloistered monks played hardly any part on either side, and even the more conservative of contemporaries were inclined to dismiss the

[1] Scotch broth

possibility that monasteries could continue in their traditional form. It was very different, it must be said, with the August-inian and Premonstratensian canons, who produced support-ers of the Reformation movement from almost its earliest years and who in large numbers passed into the ranks of the ministry of the reformed church.

The second phase of development in the medieval period, following on that of the abbeys, had been the rise of the various orders of friars. First the Dominicans, or Black Friars, and the Franciscans, or Grey Friars, founded houses in a great many towns up and down the country; Carmelites, or White Friars, followed, mainly in the late thirteenth century and the fourteenth, and then came a second series of Franciscan found-ations, of the reformed Observant rule, extending through the fifteenth century. The work of the friars lay not in the clois-tered seclusion of an abbey but in the busy world of men, where they acted as preachers and confessors. They were in some sense mobile evangelists, who reached people upon whom the more conventional elements in the church had made little impression, and the movement was an instance of 'the church going out to the people'. The friaries seem to have retained more vitality than the monasteries. As they were still attracting fresh endowments so late as the middle of the six-teenth century it can be inferred that they were in a fairly healthy state. Friars were still active as preachers and theo-logians, and with the onset of the Reformation they played a prominent part on both sides. As to their morals, the indust-rious Scottish scholar who worked out the statistics of clerical immorality[1] could not find a single legitimation of the child of a friar. Nor did they become wealthy; but as professional mendicants they acquired a reputation for greed which be-came proverbial; there was a striking enough contrast between their comfort and the condition of the genuine poor; and, whenever feeling ran high, their houses, situated in burghs, were targets for zealously Protestant burgesses as well as for riff-raff in search of loot.

[1] David Hay Fleming, *The Reformation of Scotland*, 1910.

However, by the fifteenth century it had come to be thought that new organizations should be tried, and new fashions in ecclesiastical endowment arose, suggestive of a movement away from the religious orders altogether. The typical foundation of this period was the collegiate church, where a number of priests and choristers were established to say numerous masses for the souls of the founder and his family and to maintain the services in a dignified manner. Some of these collegiate churches were quite new institutions, like Rosslyn Chapel and Trinity College in Edinburgh, others were former parish churches raised to collegiate status, like Crail and Haddington. In the same period the burgesses, whose wealth seems to have been rapidly increasing, were giving lavishly to their town churches, enlarging and adorning the fabric and endowing additional chaplainries. Fine examples are St Michael's, Linlithgow, and Holy Rude, Stirling. Another, and very important, novel feature of the period was the foundation of universities at three of the episcopal seats. St Andrews, where teaching had started in 1410 and the bishop had formally erected a university in 1412, received its bull of foundation from 'Scotland's Pope', Benedict XIII, and owed its origin to the Schism, which made it difficult for Scottish students to be accepted in countries adhering to a different Pope. Glasgow was founded in 1451, Aberdeen in 1495. (Edinburgh was a post-Reformation foundation, in 1582.) Institutions like St Salvator's College at St Andrews and King's College, Aberdeen, were at once collegiate churches and educational establishments.

The predominance of ultra-Protestant opinions in Scotland, which have been responsible for so much misinterpretation of the medieval period, have made some so critical that they have regarded that period as a kind of intrusive episode, quite barren of good and contributing nothing to the ecclesiastical tradition of the nation. Such critics have, for one thing, forgotten Scotland's debt to the medieval church for preserving essentials. It is true, for example, that knowledge of the Bible was not then as readily available as in the reformed church; but printing was not introduced to Scotland at all until the beginning of the sixteenth century, and in any event not many lay people could read. It is true, too, that people did not hear the whole of the Bible read in church, and that the portions which they did hear were read in Latin. Yet the Scriptures in their entirety were preserved, and handed on to later generations. It is also true that vernacular verse paraphrases of parts of the Bible circulated, perhaps to an extent far greater than the surviving evidence can demonstrate, and they made the substance of the gospel narrative familiar to many people, while there were religious plays which in Scotland as in England impressed vividly on the popular mind the whole cycle of the creation, the fall and redemption. It is also to be presumed that the walls of churches were adorned with paintings which kept some of the essentials of Christian teaching before the people. The methods and practices of the medieval church must be viewed in the light of the needs of a society in which, since literacy was not general, the emphasis was always on symbolism: a good deal of the ceremonial, which may well be condemned as superfluous by modern standards, was appropriate in an age when information was so often conveyed not by the written or printed word but by some symbol, like the mortar and pestle which have survived outside a chemist's shop and the striped pole outside a barber's, and when, to take another example, the essential element in the sale of land was not a written deed but the symbolic action of the delivery of earth and stone by the seller to the purchaser. Again, many medieval popular notions, and perhaps even doctrines sometimes officially expounded, may have represented elaboration or distortion of the essential Christian faith, as in the computation of the efficacy of masses and in some of the teaching about indulgences. Yet the creeds, in their primitive simplicity, were not displaced. In a similar way, the medieval church preserved the Sacraments. In their administration they might be overlaid by practices difficult to justify, and surrounded by popular misconceptions, yet our Lord's commands to baptize in the

threefold name and to commemorate Him in the Sacrament
of His Body and Blood were faithfully observed.

There is not a great deal of evidence to illustrate either the
theology or the devotional life of medieval Scotland. But two
examples may be mentioned, one from near the beginning,
the other from near the end, of the period. Upwards of eighty
sermons by Adam, who was Abbot of Dryburgh from 1184
to 1188, are extant. Adam's theological reasoning was founded
not on ecclesiastical authority, but directly on the Bible,
among the books of which he moved with ease and from
which he quoted freely; it has been noted that devotion to the
Eucharist and to the Blessed Virgin played only a small part
in his thought, and his latest biographer has remarked on the
similarity between Adam's language and that of evangelical
Protestants.[1] From a much later period we have a collection
of *Devotional pieces in verse and prose*.[2] These 'pieces' are not
by any means all original Scottish compositions, but this does
not make them less significant, and two of the most important
of them—'The contemplation of sinners' and 'The passion of
Christ' (which is a vigorous and often moving metrical para-
phrase of the gospel narrative)—are of Scottish origin. In
these documents we have the eternal essence of Christianity,
the everlasting cry of the sinner for the mediation of Christ,
and trust in redemption through His passion. A great deal of
the material in this collection, as in Adam of Dryburgh's sermons, could be used in any church, at any time.

But the merits of the medieval church have to be weighed
in the balance against flagrant defects. Its continued, and
indeed constantly renewed, vitality had found expression at
different times in bishoprics, abbeys, friaries, collegiate churches, cathedrals and universities, but it had neglected the
service of the parish churches. Indeed, the successive developments had been detrimental to the parishes, for the whole
ecclesiastical structure was very largely financed at their
expense, through a process known as 'appropriation'. Tithes,

---

[1] James Bulloch, *Adam of Dryburgh*, 1958.
[2] Published by the Scottish Text Society in 1955.

or teinds as they are called in Scotland, were tenths of produce of every kind, collected to provide funds for the maintenance of a priest to serve the parish church. But by the 'appropriation' of parishes the bulk of the teinds of an overwhelming majority of the Scottish parishes came to be diverted to the maintenance of a cathedral, a bishopric, an abbey or some other institution, and in every parish where this happened the parochial work was committed to an underpaid vicar. A minimum stipend for vicars had been fixed in the thirteenth century at 10 merks (£6 13s 4d), tardily raised to 20 and 24 merks in the sixteenth century. But by that time a reasonable competence for a professional man was somewhere in the region of £80 to £100 a year, in the Scots money of the time, and few vicars can have had a living wage. It is plain that one great indictment of the medieval church is that it was top-heavy. Its resources were concentrated at the higher levels, which were maintained at the expense of the parishes. Our admiration of the remains of splendid medieval cathedrals and abbeys should be tempered by a recollection of the impoverishment of the parishes which those institutions represented, as well as by reflection on pre-Reformation neglect and the imbalance between ecclesiastical wealth and the condition of the poor. And the situation was constantly deteriorating. Every collegiate church founded, every new canonry in a cathedral, every university college, drained off more and more money which should have been supporting the ministry of the parish churches.

The underpayment of the parish clergy had results, direct and indirect, which account for many of the more conspicuous evils in the church. Most obviously, there was more than a temptation, there was sheer necessity, for a vicar either to accumulate several livings or to engage in some secular occupation, for only thus could he hope to make ends meet, and in either event the sacred functions were bound to be imperfectly performed. Less directly, the diversion of revenues from the parishes affected the intellectual and moral standards of the clergy. They could hardly be other than ill-educated, for no man of ability or learning was likely to accept the starvation wages paid to the vicars. Their poor educational level meant in turn that they were more likely to indulge in carnal than in intellectual recreations. The registers which record the legitimations of clerical offspring, and which disclose so little to the discredit of monks and friars, give the names of hundreds of children of secular clergy.

But if evils, material and moral, followed from the poverty of the parochial clergy, evils flowed equally from its counterpart, the wealth of the dignitaries, who were superior to the vicars in their educational attainments but not in their morals or their regard for discipline. It was not, as a matter of fact, the poorly paid vicars who were most conspicuous as pluralists; it was careerists who piled one fat canonry or dignity upon another until they accumulated an income surpassing that of some bishops. Again, while vicarages did sometimes remain in a family and even pass from father to son, this abuse too was more conspicuous in the higher ranges of the ecclesiastical structure. 'The kin'—blood relationship—has always been a potent element in Scottish life, and the wealthier the benefice the less inclination was there to let it go out of the family. In several benefices, more particularly cathedral prebends, members of the same family succeeded generation by generation.

It is abundantly clear, therefore, that extremes of wealth and poverty alike led to irregularities. But they need not have done so, and would not have done so, had they not been accompanied by a general relaxation of discipline throughout the whole church. If neglect of the parishes was one major defect, lack of discipline was another.

Discipline should in the first place have included the operation of machinery which would control appointments and restrict them to suitable candidates. But after a long contest between the Pope and the king over the right to appoint to the greater benefices, the crown's right, first of recommendation, later of nomination, was conceded, and the result was a series of scandalous appointments, beginning in the reign of James IV, who appointed first his brother, aged twenty-one, and then his illegitimate son, aged eleven, to the archbishopric of St Andrews. Worse was to come. James V, at the age of twenty, wrote to the Pope, remarking on the frailty of human nature and intimating that he had three small sons, for whose welfare he was, out of his paternal affection, much concerned. He asked the Pope to grant them a dispensation to be promoted to any office whatever in the church; the only restriction was that they were not to be bishops or archbishops until they reached the age of twenty. The Pope, as it happened, was Clement VII, who is known to some historians as the upholder of Christian morality against Henry VIII. But—even although one of James's sons was the issue of an adulterous connection—Pope Clement gave the king of Scots a free hand to distribute Scotland's wealthiest abbeys among his illegitimate offspring. Reflection on the vanished glories of Kelso, Melrose, St Andrews, Holyrood and Coldingham should not exclude a recollection of what the Pope allowed the king to do with those places.

So far as lesser benefices were concerned, there were other defects both in admission and oversight. Episcopal authority and discipline generally were undermined through the system of dispensations, by which canon law was constantly being set aside. Any bishop who might have wished to suppress irregularities in his diocese would have been thwarted by papal action. His control over appointments in his diocese had largely been taken from him through the system of appointment at Rome; no attempt to keep unsuitable clergy out of the diocese could succeed; any effort to check non-residence or pluralism could be defied by those who could flourish papal dispensations in his face and flout his authority; and it was futile to try to deal with unchastity if a priest's bastard could obtain a dispensation enabling him to succeed his father in his benefice. Equally, the Scottish provincial council could and did pass well-intentioned statutes against irregularities, only to find that these statutes could not be enforced when Rome itself was not upholding canon law. Contemporaries were well aware that dispensations might nullify attempts at reform, and that to that extent the papacy was an obstacle to discipline and good government.

One of the recurrent difficulties of the medieval church was the maintenance of its buildings. The ambitions of architects and benefactors often outran their resources, with the result that a number of churches—especially collegiate churches—were never completed, and others were structurally unsound. The wars with England resulted in successive devastations of churches, in the Lothians and the Borders especially, and apart from foreign invasion there was civil war and disorder, accidental damage from fire and lightning. But there were other, more avoidable, factors at work. As men's zeal declined, they were unwilling to see their revenues used in the repair of church buildings; and the financial starvation of the parishes accounts in part for the shameful condition of some churches and their furnishings, reflected in the repeated legislation of provincial councils, from the thirteenth century to the sixteenth, urging the repair of ruinous churches. When the Archbishop of St Andrews visited the churches of Berwickshire in 1556, he found, he said, that the walls of some were levelled to the ground, in others the walls or roofs were threatening collapse, many were without windows to keep out the weather, some were without fonts, without altar vestments, even without missals, so that mass could not be celebrated. A special report on the church of Ayton, which was unhappily situated on the main east coast route into Scotland from the south, said that it had recently been re-roofed, though only with turf and thatch, as it was not thought worth while to put on a better roof 'for fear of the Englishmen'; but the new roof lasted less than a year, whereupon a canopy was erected over the high altar to shelter the priest and the clerk in wet weather; and when it was fine, the report goes on, mass was said 'whiles [sometimes] at the Lady altar and whiles in the kirk yaird'.

What the effect of all this may have been on the general

level of church life it is easier to guess than to demonstrate from record evidence. Church attendance and the standard of devotion had probably all along been adversely affected by the lack of an adequate number of churches in some rural areas and the distance of many homes from a place of worship, for Scotland suffered from a chronic shortage of churches until so late as the nineteenth century, when intense ecclesiastical competition at last provided a more than adequate supply. There were complaints in 1552 that very few people were attending church at all. And even when they did come to church, their conduct left much to be desired. The authorities fulminated against 'hearing mass irreverently and impiously', against 'carrolling and wanton singing in the kirk' and against those who, in time of divine service, occupied themselves with 'jesting and behaving scurrilously' or 'talking, laughing, scorning and suchlike doings'. The inside of a church clearly commanded little respect, and narratives of deeds of violence in churches have as their stock phrase such words as 'with no honour to the most holy Sacrament'. Neither persons nor property secured safety by seeking the protection of the sanctuary and it was not unknown for a priest to be dragged from the very altar in pursuance of some private feud.

One of the features of the medieval church which is apt to be idealized is the association of the church with the everyday life of the people. The parish church fulfilled functions which today belong to the radio, the theatre, the newspaper, the local government offices, council chamber, law courts and social centre. It is believed that the church permeated the whole of life to an extent unknown today. But it can be argued that this situation led as much to the secularization of the church as to the sanctification of the world. It was not altogether healthy that the hours of divine service, when a congregation could be expected to gather, were considered the most suitable time for the various secular activities conducted in the sacred edifice. There is not the slightest doubt that attention to the proper functions of the church was constantly distracted by thoughts of worldly affairs, and that was partly why church buildings were treated with scant respect.

If standards were low throughout the country generally, they were worse in the western Highlands and islands. There were hardy any religious houses at all in the entire Highland area, and the cathedrals for Highland sees were all planted in the part of the diocese nearest the Lowlands, except in the west, where they were on islands. If the aim was security, it was not achieved. The cathedral of Elgin was burned by raiders in 1390, those of Dunblane and Dornoch were said to be ruinous in the 1420s. At Dunkeld, when the bishop was celebrating mass one Whitsunday, the cathedral was attacked by armed men and he had to take refuge in the rafters above the choir; and it was for a time the custom to hold the diocesan synod not at Dunkeld but in the safety of a friary on the outskirts of Perth, on account, so it was said, of the ferocity of the Highland robbers against churchmen. Bishops who ventured into the west Highlands and islands were apt to find that they were unwelcome, and the Bishop of Argyll obtained leave for seven years to administer his diocese not, like his brother of Dunkeld, from a safe place within it, but from the more remote security of Glasgow. There were such long vacancies in the sees of Argyll and the Isles that, as we are told in 1529, those born in the more remote islands had not had baptism or other sacrament, not to speak of Christian teaching. The facts provide but a slender foundation on which to build the romantic fiction of a pious Catholic populace who maintained their faith uncontaminated by the Reformation.

The discreditable state of the Scottish church before the Reformation is a sombre, indeed a sordid, topic, a part of his national history on which no Scot can look back with any satisfaction, still less with pride. That the picture has remained a familiar one is due partly to the fact that it was described in contemporary writings which had a great popular appeal in their own day and later and some of which are of great literary merit—works like Sir David Lindsay's *Satire of the Three Estates*, a drama originally produced in 1540 and revived with extraordinary success in recent times at the Edinburgh Festival, and John Knox's *History of the Reformation*, a most spirited narrative of the period from the pen of a principal actor in it. Possibly too many accounts of the state of the church have relied on such sources, and so have been open to the criticism that they were citing as authorities works which either were frankly partisan or were works of art rather than of verity. But the fact is that every line of the denunciations of the ecclesiastical system in Lindsay's works can be documented from record evidence. Moreover, the councils of the clergy themselves legislated against precisely the abuses which the reformers described, and alluded to the 'profane lewdness of life in churchmen of almost all ranks, together with crass ignorance of literature and of all the liberal arts.' A Scottish priest, writing to the Archbishop of St Andrews, complained that men were 'ordained to handle the Lord's sacred Body who hardly knew their alphabet'. A cardinal wrote to the Pope describing the shamelessness of the nuns, who 'defile the sacred precincts with the birth of children, go forth abroad surrounded by their numerous sons, and give their daughters in marriage dowered with the ample revenues of the church', and added: 'Very many churches and monasteries had been established of old in stately buildings, but within the last ten years or thereabouts had been reduced to ruins by hostile inroads, or through the avarice and neglect of those placed in charge are crumbling to decay.' And a Jesuit envoy reported to his superior that one cause of the church's decay was that 'benefices are constantly bestowed on children, and on absolutely unworthy persons. . . . The second case is the lives of priests and clerics, which are extremely licentious and scandalous; and a third cause is the absolutely supine negligence of the bishops. . . . It is no wonder that, with such shepherds, the wolves invade the flock of the Lord, and ruin all.' No contemporary, whatever his views, attempted to palliate the abuses, and it is somewhat futile for anyone in the twentieth century to attempt to deny them.

The medieval system could, at its best, provide for the worship of God in splendid cathedrals, abbeys and collegiate churches and for the saying of prayers and masses for the living and the dead at countless altars, but it could not provide adequate ministrations for the congregations of the parish churches. Not only did they lack the instruction and the preaching which a properly trained secular clergy could have provided, but they did not even enjoy satisfactory administration of the sacramental services to which contemporary thought attached most importance. There is little documentary support for the idealized view of the Middle Ages as 'the ages of faith', when a high standard of spiritual fervour was steadily maintained. Regrets are sometimes expressed that the Scottish church has produced few 'saints' since the Reformation, but it is not irrelevant to observe that the whole of the medieval period enriched the Scottish Kalendar with only three names—Queen Margaret, who was English, Earl Magnus of Orkney, who was Scandinavian, and Bishop Gilbert of Caithness, who alone of the three was, presumably, a native.

D

5

THE REFORMATION

THE beginning of the Reformation on the continent of Europe is dated from Luther's attack on indulgences in 1517, and in England Henry VIII established his supremacy over the church in 1534. In Scotland, 'the Reformation' is dated in 1560, but from as early as 1525, when there was an Act of Parliament against the import of Lutheran literature, there had been a series of incidents—especially trials of 'heretics' and attacks on ecclesiastical properties— generally indicative of the spread of reforming opinions. As 'the Reformation' of 1560 did not come without warning, the Scottish church had had ample time to reform itself without waiting for revolution. The situation was not wholly desperate, for in the 1540s and 1550s conventional piety still found expression in the endowment of chaplainries, in gifts to the friars, in the foundation of collegiate churches and in the organization of university colleges. Not only so, but efforts at reform, designed to avert drastic changes, were made. Under the primacy of John Hamilton, who was not opposed to doctrinal modification in a Lutheran direction, three councils of the Scottish church, in 1549, 1552 and 1559, passed a whole code of reforming statutes. There was to be strict examination of ordinands and of the clergy already in possession of benefices, regular visitation by bishops in person, more preaching and instruction, and repair of church buildings. A lot of this was not likely to be taken seriously when the bishops, from John Hamilton downwards, showed little sign of reforming their own lives. However, in a sense the most serious weakness of this programme lay in its failure to provide the improved

finance at parochial level which was so essential. What was
required—and this the more radical reformers clearly saw—
was a drastic redistribution of endowments, so that the claims
of the parishes should come first and not last. The wealth of
of the church, if applied primarily to parochial purposes,
could have given each parish something like £300 per annum
and still left plenty over to pay for regional and central organization. But all that Archbishop Hamilton proposed to do was
to raise the minimum stipend to 20 or 24 merks.

What was happening, in the absence of any official scheme
for the redistribution of endowments, was a vast amount of
unofficial redistribution, of a kind which did not help the
church. The crown was making inroads on the church's
wealth, partly by having scions of the royal house endowed
with wealthy abbeys, partly by direct taxation. And, through
the charters of church lands and leases of tithes which ecclesi-
astics granted in profusion in the years before 1560, the nobility and gentry were likewise recovering much of the wealth
which their ancestors had lavished on religious foundations.

The period which produced the policy of reform from
within saw also a sharp decline of papal power in Scotland.
The crown was not now content merely to nominate men for
appointment by the Pope, but was tending to make appointments without reference to Rome at all. Archbishop Hamilton,
too, had powers, as a legate, which enabled him to exercise
many functions previously performed at Rome, and the Pope
in the end relinquished his control over the alienation of
ecclesiastical property. All in all, the papacy was well on the
way to being eliminated from Scottish ecclesiastical machinery.
And there was an accompanying tendency to disregard the
papacy in theory. Attention has often been drawn to the fact
that the Catechism issued by Archbishop Hamilton, in 1552,
is silent about the Pope—only one of several particulars in
which it showed a readiness to meet the reformers half-way.
Statements by the provincial council and by the conservative
writer Quentin Kennedy are explicit on the authority in doctrine of 'the Church' or 'general councils', but likewise ignore

the papacy. The record of the Popes being what it was, men may well have felt that no help could be expected from Rome, and certainly when the crisis came the Pope was to have few friends in Scotland, even among those otherwise conservative in their views. Not only, therefore, is the apparent suddenness of the Reformation in Scotland very largely an illusion, but the proceedings of Henry VIII, who cast off the papacy but retained the traditional theology and polity, are not entirely without parallel in the 'Hamiltonian papacy' represented by the administration of James Hamilton, Earl of Arran, as governor of the realm, and his brother John, as archbishop and legate. There was undoubtedly a party, or at least a body of opinion, in Scotland, which looked to a reformed catholicism, national or non-papal.

The national element in the Reformation could hardly be other than conspicuous, and not only or even mainly in relation to the papacy, for international politics played a large part in shaping the situation. Warfare between Scotland and England had often been renewed since Edward I's attempt at conquest, and Scotland had been the constant ally of France. But in the sixteenth century, after the defeat at Flodden (1513) many Scots came to realize that continued hostility to England, and the use of their country as the tool of France, could lead only to disaster. This disposition to reconsider Anglo-Scottish relations on political grounds was reinforced by religious motives after Henry VIII broke with Rome and Scottish reformers began to see in England a possible ally, while England on her side fostered the reforming movement in Scotland partly for the political end of detaching Scotland from France. The issue between the two Scottish factions—one favourable to the Reformation and looking for support to England, the other conservative in religion and upholding the old alliance with France—remained uncertain throughout the 1540s and 1550s, partly because there were impolitic invasions by the English which alienated the Scots and threw patriotic sentiment on to the side of France, and partly because during the Roman Catholic reaction under Mary

Tudor (1553–8) England was no friend to Scottish Protestants. Decision came when new factors emerged to reverse the situation, and one of those factors was Scottish fear of French domination. Mary, Queen of Scots, who had succeeded her father in 1543 at the age of one week, had been sent to France in 1548 to be brought up as the prospective bride of the heir to the French throne, and in her absence Scotland was governed (from 1554) by her mother, Mary of Guise, a Frenchwoman. French forces garrisoned Scottish fortresses, Frenchmen occupied high offices. Should Queen Mary become queen of France, Scotland would be ruled by her descendants, who would be kings of France, and Scotland would simply be absorbed into the French monarchy. In consequence, resentment against the French began to strengthen the reformed cause, which thus became the national cause. But this political situation was at the same time decisive against the possibility that a reformation would be carried through in Scotland with the countenance of the lawful sovereign. Quite apart from the personal views of Mary of Guise, her administration was subordinate to the policy of France, a country which had rejected the Reformation, and her object was to ensure that her daughter and her heirs would rule both France and Scotland. If there was to be a reformation in Scotland, theefore, it could come about only as a result of a political revolution and in defiance of the crown.

The revolution came about in 1559 and 1560. The marriage of Queen Mary to the Dauphin (April 1558) intensified the fear of French domination; under Elizabeth Tudor, who became queen of England in November 1558, England might once more give help to the Scottish reformers against France and Rome; and John Knox reappeared in Scotland in May 1559. Knox (?1511–1572) had been associated in 1547 with a revolutionary group who had seized St Andrews castle after murdering Archbishop David Betoun, and, when the castle fell to the French, he had been sent as a prisoner to the French galleys. After his release he had spent several years mainly in England and on the continent, and it was from Geneva that he now returned to stimulate the reformers by his preaching. Attacks on some religious houses were followed by military operations conducted by Knox's noble and baronial allies, known as the 'Lords of the Congregation', who in October 1559 formally suspended Mary of Guise from the government and in the spring of 1560, with English help, drove out the French. This point marks the end of the war with England which had gone intermittently for nearly three hundred years, and a diplomatic revolution which ended the Auld Alliance with France and established a new alliance with the southern neighbour which had for so long been the Auld Enemy. John Knox, reformer and friend to England, enemy to France and Rome, prayed that there might never more be war between England and Scotland, and his prayer was answered.

In August 1560 a Parliament met which abrogated the authority of the Pope in Scotland, adopted a reformed Confession of Faith and forbade the celebration of the Latin mass. But although the absent Queen Mary had authorized the meeting of this Parliament, it had been forbidden to deal with religion, its composition was irregular and its legislation was not confirmed by the queen. Mary returned to Scotland from France in August 1561, and for the next six years, until she was deposed and superseded by her infant son, James VI, the reformed church was in an ambiguous and precarious legal situation.

The new church system which the reformers proposed in 1560 to substitute for the old was one which had its basis in a new emphasis on the service of the parishes. The primary requirements of the reformers were that 'the Word' should be preached and the Sacraments duly administered, and this could be achieved only if the top-heavy superstructure of the church should be abolished or modified and the balance redressed in favour of the parishes. The Reformation was in any event anti-monastic, and it was critical of cathedrals and collegiate churches, monuments as they were to the neglect of the cure of souls. If, then, the monasteries, friaries and collegiate churches were stripped of their wealth, and the parishes regained the revenues which properly belonged to them, a competent ministry could be maintained throughout the land, ministers and their flocks could be educated, churches could be decently maintained. The structure of the parish ministry was determined by the reformers' stress on Word and Sacraments and the balance between the two. Ministers were qualified both to preach and to administer the Sacraments; exhorters were authorized to preach but could not administer the Sacraments; and readers were permitted only to read the 'common prayers' from a service-book, the lessons from the Bible, and homilies from the Book of Homilies. The intermediate office of exhorter had a short life, and its disappearance is probably to be related to a change which in 1572 raised the status of readers by authorizing them to officiate at baptisms and marriages and so, probably designedly, made their office akin to that of the Anglican deacon.

Proposals for organization and finance at parochial level were not in themselves sufficient to ensure that the Word would be preached and the Sacraments administered. The parish clergy would require supervision, and the reaction against relaxed discipline involved a reform of the machinery for oversight. The reformers had no use for the defective episcopate with which they were so familiar, nor did they believe in a personal succession, whether through bishops or through presbyters. It is less than fair to them to say that they broke 'the succession', because when they looked at the inefficient, immoral and persecuting prelates of the old order they considered it to be demonstrable that 'the succession' had already lapsed. The belief of the reformers was in a succession of truth, their emphasis was on faith and on works, which were the test of the true pastor and the true bishop alike; but none of them—not even Calvin —was opposed to episcopacy in the sense that supervision of the lower clergy should be carried out by individuals of higher rank, each responsible for a district or diocese. Bishops of a kind there were to be, bishops sound in doctrine and energetic in their duties of supervising, visiting, organizing and preaching. Bishops were no longer to be frustrated by dispensations from Rome, they were no longer to be diverted from their pastoral work by political and courtly duties. One aspect of the Reformation was actually the restoration of an episcopate after its depression by papal action, its revival in an administrative sense by liberating bishops from their entanglement in politics. Not only so, but whereas in the middle ages the office of bishop had not been one of the seven orders of clergy, the episcopate was now integrated in a 'three-fold ministry' of bishop, priest and deacon.

Where were the reformed bishops to come from? There was no possibility of bringing any compulsion to bear on the existing bishops to make them accept the Reformation. In England, where the crown was able to make the bishops, and indeed all the clergy, choose between accepting the Reformation and losing their offices, the great majority chose to accept the Reformation, while those who declined were simply removed and replaced by reformers, so that the entire structure of ecclesiastical administration continued without change. But in Scotland the crown was on the other side, and the 'Lords of the Congregation', whose administration was only a provisional government of uncertain constitutional status, could not deal with the bishops of Scotland as Queen Elizabeth had dealt with those of England, more especially as most of the Scottish bishops were members of powerful families whom the Scottish reformers dared not offend.

Compulsion being impossible, persuasion was tried, but with only imperfect success. Only one of the bishops was wholly intransigent, and he lost no time in making for France; the majority were hesitant, because they had a preference for what they regarded as catholicism, although they had no great love for the papacy and no desire to incur inconvenience, still less martyrdom; four gave unqualified support to the reformers, and three of the four continued to administer their dioceses and advanced the cause of the Reformation within them. Scotland was later on to boast that it had 'reformed from popery by presbyters', but that was an injustice to the bishops who carried through the Reformation in the dioceses of Galloway, Orkney and Caithness. The acceptance of those bishops into the reformed church supports the view that it was political accident which compelled the Scots generally to dispense with bishops in 1560.

As the existing episcopate could not in general continue in the reformed church, a substitute had to be found. The first *Book of Discipline*, in which Knox and some of his colleagues defined their programme for polity and endowment, proposed that the regional administration of the church should be in the hands of ten superintendents. To contemporaries 'superintendent' was a familiar term, connoting the whole ideal of the 'godly' or reformed bishop, but the office has been misunderstood by posterity. Presbyterians dislike the superintendents because they infringed the parity of ministers, while Episcopalians have dismissed them because they were not consecrated bishops, and errors have multiplied: the superintendents, it has been said, had no superiority over their brethren, they had no special honour accorded to them, their office had no great pecuniary advantage, they normally held parochial charges as well as having their diocesan work, and their office was designed as a temporary expedient pending the erection of presbyteries—and all of those assertions are untrue. The superintendent was superior to ministers in legislative, judicial and administrative functions: unlike ministers, he had the right to attend every general assembly; he presided over a court with extensive authority; he alone could authorize the admission of ministers to their charges, and his powers of oversight extended not only to visitation and inspection, but to correction. He was styled *dominus superintendens* or 'my lord superintendent' and enjoyed a salary much above that of most ministers and comparable with that of some contemporary bishops. No more than five superintendents were appointed, partly indeed because there was no need for them in dioceses where the bishops had conformed and partly because there seems to have been some hesitation about appointing them in dioceses where there were still hopes that the bishop might come over—but largely because the reformed church found the office of superintendent far too expensive. In some districts, therefore, ministers were given commissions to do some of the work of superintendents, in addition to their own parochial work, in return for a comparatively small fee. An episcopal, or quasi-episcopal, system, it must always be remembered, was an expensive system which needy—or greedy—Scots thought they could not afford; it is no mere gibe to say that presbyterianism was later to make its appeal to the Scots partly because it was cheap, and it has not yet lost that appeal today.

In course of time, when Queen Mary was deposed to make way for her young son, James VI, the government was on the side of the reformed church and the political situation was like that in England. The financial difficulty about maintaining superintendents could now be overcome, or circumvented, for in 1572 it was arranged that ministers should be appointed to bishoprics as they fell vacant, to exercise the powers of superintendents. The belief that those bishops were no more than instruments to divert church property to the crown and the nobility, and the quaint comparison of them to 'tulchans' —a 'tulchan' being a calf's skin stuffed with straw and placed beside a cow to make her give milk—have gone far to obscure their real significance. Whatever their financial dealings, those bishops were clerics, inaugurated by a rite of 'consecration' which, though not in accordance with Anglican standards, represented an attempt to give them a respectable spiritual lineage, and they took their due place in ecclesiastical administration. They were 'titular' bishops only in the sense that they were not in the 'apostolic succession' as Anglicans understand it. This jargon about 'tulchans' and 'titulars' has concealed the important fact that, once political circumstances allowed it, the Scots followed English example and took over the old structure of the bishoprics. An episcopate without 'the succession' on the one hand but equally without any doctrine of parity on the other was of course paralleled in some of the Lutheran churches, and indeed the whole ecclesiastical polity of Scotland in that period has a strong Lutheran flavour about it.

Contemporaries were in no doubt that the office of bishop or superintendent was not only expedient—indeed essential —but that it had divine sanction. 'Without the care of super-intendents,' it was pronounced in a formal document, 'neither can the kirks be suddenly erected, neither can they be retained in discipline and unity of doctrine. Of Christ Jesus and his apostles we have command and example to appoint men to such charges.'[1] And again, 'To take away the office of bishop were to take away the order which God hath appointed in his church.'[2] These are the words of Scottish reformers, words of the colleagues of John Knox. And Knox himself, who had sent his own sons south to be educated for the ministry of the Church of England, gave as his farewell advice to the Church of Scotland that it should faithfully and fully imple-ment the plan of 1572 and so have more bishops and better bishops.[3]

If the Reformation was thus in a very real sense a reaction in favour of an episcopate, it was also a reaction in favour of the laity. They were to be raised through education, learning was to be no monopoly of a priestly caste, and an instructed people were to have a part in church affairs from which they had previously been excluded. The new emphasis is con-spicuous in the changes which the reformers made in public worship. The vernacular was substituted for Latin, metrical psalms were introduced and service books were put into the hands of the people, so that all could take part. The non-communicating mass was abolished and in its place came a corporate action in which the participation of the people was essential. It proved impracticable to achieve the ideal of making a celebration of Holy Communion the centre of wor-ship every Sunday, because the people, so long accustomed to communicate only once a year, declined to come frequently, while the ministers, on their side, declined to celebrate with only a few communicants. But although there could not be

[1] *St Andrews Kirk Session Register*, I (Scottish History Society 4, 1888), p. 75.
[2] Calderwood, *History of the Church of Scotland* (Wodrow Society), III, 158.
[3] *Ibid.*, III, 765–7.

an actual celebration every Sunday, or anything like every Sunday, the reformers did what they thought the next best thing by adopting as the centre of the Sunday morning worship those parts of the Communion service which did not directly concern the celebration. In England too, at that time, celebrations were comparatively rare, and the usual service consisted, as the Prayer Book directed, of the Commandments, the Collect, Epistle and Gospel, the Creed, Sermon, Offertory and Prayer for the Church. In Scotland likewise there can be discerned in the Sunday morning service the general structure of the first part of the Communion service, concluding, like the English service, with a long intercession after sermon. There could be no mistake about the intention to uphold the Communion service as the norm of Sunday morning worship. When the service was completed by an actual celebration, it was one in which the cup was restored to the laity and in which ministers and communicants assembled round a table. It followed further from the raising of the status of the laity that the appeal in worship could be less to the emotions and more to the intellect, for with education the need for symbolism would vanish and a great deal of the ceremonial which had been designed for an illiterate medieval populace would become superfluous.

The raising of the status of the laity, when applied to church order, issued in the anti-clericalism which was such a marked feature of the reformers' system. The clergy were no longer to claim exemption from the authority of the state, and control over the clergy and laity alike was to rest with the Christian community or its representatives. Normally, where the reformed church obtained recognition from the state, supreme authority over the church would rest with the crown, as happened in Lutheran countries and in England, but exceptionally such authority might lie with the estates of the realm or with lesser magistrates, and that is what happened at first in Scotland. Church and Nation were then co-terminous; each consisted of the same people, each was coextensive with the whole population, church and state were but different aspects of one and the same society. There was plainly no need, therefore, to set up any separate organ to represent lay authority over the church, for the organs of government responsible for the state would naturally be responsible for the church as well. The fact that the papacy had rejected the call for reformation meant also that, in every country where ecclesiastical revolution came about, it had to be carried through on a national basis. Not only did the crown or other organs of civil government inevitably take the lead, but it was with such official support alone that papal authority could be abrogated and the bishops and other holders of church property be brought either to accept the Reformation or to relinquish their benefices to others. In Scotland as elsewhere the reformers looked to the crown for leadership and repeatedly urged the sovereign to carry through a programme of reform. Only when 'the prince' failed to do his duty did the reformers turn to other constitutional organs.

It is in this appeal to the laity, to the magistracy, and not in any claim to ecclesiastical independence, that the origins of the General Assembly are to be found. Mary, Queen of Scots, who went to mass, could not be supreme head on earth of the Church of Scotland, and neither her council nor her parliament could be permitted to exercise ecclesiastical authority. The substitute for the royal supremacy, which the Scots could not have, was found in a general assembly consisting of representatives of the same three estates of the realm which at that time formed a Scottish parliament—barons, burgesses and clergy. Lords and barons attended these assemblies in considerable numbers, but as individuals and not because they were elders of the kirk or representatives of congregations or other ecclesiastical organs; burgh commissioners attended, appointed not by any ecclesiastical body but by the town councils; and the clerical element consisted of the superintendents along with a selected number of ministers. In such an assembly, which was not an essentially clerical body, we have the 'godly estates', the substitute for the 'godly prince' whom the Scots did not have. That this is a true reading of the situation would seem to be confirmed by what happened after 1567, when there was at last a 'godly prince' in Scotland who was acknowledged as 'supreme governor of the realm as well in things temporal as in the conservation and purgation of religion', and when it was seriously contended that the General Assembly should come to an end as no longer necessary. It was plainly difficult to justify the existence of such a body when the same elements were assembled in a parliament which was now equally 'godly', and there were some who considered that the assembly had been nothing more than a temporary expedient, pending the accession of a 'godly prince'.

And if the General Assembly thus represents anti-clericalism in central government, anti-clericalism was equally strong at congregational level. Congregations were to elect their ministers, and the concept seems to have been that ministerial authority ascended from the congregation and did not descend from the bishop or superintendent, although the latter had to examine and admit the congregation's nominee. The kirk session equally represented an element of lay control, an element of anti-clericalism. It was an important distinction from the practice and the theory of the later, presbyterian, system, that elders and deacons were at first elected annually. There was no possibility of mistaking such elders and deacons for an order of the ministry, for they were manifestly laymen, and these genuinely lay elders could examine, censure and (with the superintendent's sanction) even depose their minister. Anti-clericalism could hardly go further. In view of the obviously lay nature of the elder's office in the Reformation period, it would seem that if a 'threefold ministry' is to be found in the Knoxian church the equation of bishop, priest and deacon is not to be made with minister, elder and deacon, but with superintendent, minister and reader.

The reformed Church of Scotland was no doubt 'Calvinist' in its theology, but so also was the Church of England at that time. The Scottish polity, however, was not yet 'presbyterian': the presbytery did not exist, the synod existed merely as the superintendent's diocesan synod, and both General Assembly and kirk session were different in composition and in conception from the later presbyterian organs of the same name, while the office of superintendent is irreconcilable with presbyterian theories of parity. Any resemblance to the present-day presbyterian polity is only superficial. If the reformers' system is to be characterized in modern terminology, it might perhaps be described as congregationalism with a dash of episcopacy.

From beginning to end the Scottish Reformation was marked by far less dislocation and far more continuity than is popularly believed, and by a minimum of personal rancour. In England, on Elizabeth's accession, the bishops who had held office under Mary were imprisoned, and ultra-Protestants clamoured for their blood; but in Scotland the clergy in general had at least two-thirds of their incomes secured to them for life and bishops and dignitaries continued to sit on the council, in apparent amity, alongside supporters of the Reformation. Again, there was in Scotland no dissolution of the monasteries. The abbots or commendators continued to draw their revenues, or most of them, as long as they lived; the monks were entitled to their portions and their quarters in the precincts after the Reformation as before it; and the house remained a corporation—a property-owning corporation. In this era, every form of persecution, bloodshed and cruelty was less conspicuous in Scotland than in England. The Scottish conservatives put a mere handful of 'heretics' to death, over a period of thirty-two years; and although there was a statute imposing the death penalty for saying mass (a penalty at that time attached to many trivial offences), not more than two, and very likely only one, priest suffered under it. There was nothing in Scotland to compare with the wholesale executions in England—those three hundred Protestants under Mary and those two hundred Roman Catholics under Elizabeth. Nor were there in Scotland armed rebellions, cruelly suppressed, like the 'Pilgrimage of Grace', Wyatt's Rebellion, and the Northern Rising.

Although no attempt was made in Scotland to preserve a personal succession, yet in practice the new ministry was very largely recruited from the parish priests, canons regular, monks and friars. In some areas the majority of the parish clergy continued to serve their flocks under the new regime, and in some houses of canons regular a majority of the members took part in the work of the reformed church. If there was thus personal continuity, there was also material continuity, for most of the existing buildings remained in use. Some abbeys and collegiate churches were said at the time to have been 'cast doun', but while contemporaries in England and posterity in Scotland interpreted the phrase as equivalent to 'levelled to the ground', all it can have meant was that fittings and ornaments were removed and the institution overthrown in a figurative sense, for some of the buildings so referred to were still standing in the nineteenth century. If we take into account the buildings which were partially in ruin before 1560, those which were not ruined until considerably later, and those still standing today, it emerges that the number reduced to ruin by the reformers was very inconsiderable. The truth is that the reformers inherited the results of a generation or so of neglect, dilapidation and destruction, and their concern was not to demolish buildings but to repair them so that they could be used for parochial worship. A very large number of the medieval churches remained in use until their replacement became necessary with the rapid growth of population after 1750, and a good many are still in use today. Equally, while there was much destruction in 1560 of statues and church furnishings, yet some fine work in wood and stone survived to come under the censure of covenanting General Assemblies in the 1640s, and some survived until it was removed in the course of nineteenth-century restorations. The reformers can thus be acquitted of the general and systematic destruction of churches.

It is equally true that the reformers had no peculiar responsibility for suppressing innocent pleasures and making Scotland—especially on Sundays—the dull place some visitors consider it to be. Scottish Sabbatarianism, we saw earlier, came from England (or possibly Hungary) with Queen Margaret,[1] and Archbishop Hamilton's Catechism gave instructions on Sunday observance which would today satisfy all but the most austere.[2] Dancing, which John Knox did not 'utterly condemn' (as he was careful to explain to Queen Mary), had been denounced twice over in Hamilton's Catechism as 'an occasion of sin' and a 'provocation of lechery'.[3] The first attempt to suppress the traditional May-day festivities was made by the Catholic administration of Mary of Guise.[4] A scale of fines for profanity, graded according to the social station and wealth of the offender, was to be imposed during Cromwell's administration in the middle of the seventeenth century, but it had been anticipated by the Scottish Parliament before the Reformation and was to be re-enacted after the Restoration, this time by a Parliament known as the 'Drunken Parliament'.[5] The stringency of Scottish licensing laws can be traced as far back as 1436, when persons found drinking in taverns after 9 p.m. became liable to imprisonment.[6] The reformers' policy, it may be concluded, was only one manifestation among many of an oft-recurring strain of puritanism. Kirk session discipline, which was introduced by the reformers and remained an important feature of Scottish life, throughout presbyterian and episcopalian ascendancy alike, for more than two centuries, popularly suggests a preoccupation with the exposure of sexual irregularities, and it is true that the public denunciation of offenders from the pulpit, week by week, imported into the worship of the Church of Scotland a form of Sunday entertainment which is nowadays purveyed only by the less reputable Sunday newspapers. But, in an age when

[1] See p. 18 above.

[2] Hamilton, *Catechism*, p. 68.

[3] Knox, *History of the Reformation*, ed. Dickinson, II, p. 45; Hamilton, *Catechism*, pp. 68, 91.

[4] *Acts of the Parliaments of Scotland*, II, 500.

[5] *Scotland and the Protectorate* (Scottish History Society 31, 1899), p. 404; Patrick, *Statutes of the Scottish Church* (Scottish History Society 54, 1907), p. lxxiv; *Acts of the Parliaments of Scotland*, II, 485; VII, 262.

[6] *Acts of the Parliaments of Scotland*, II, 24.

E

there was no police force, the sessions took cognisance of assault, drunkenness, profanity, slander and petty theft, and it seems more than probable that, at least where they had the weight of public opinion behind them and were backed by the local magistrates, their unremitting vigilance had far-reaching effects in inducing respect for the moral law. An age like our own, when delinquency of all kinds increasingly abounds, cannot afford to scoff at the kirk sessions.

Yet even when all error and misunderstanding have been cleared away, it remains true that few at the present day would approve every part of the reformers' programme. Their repudiation of succession and their rejection of the laying on of hands are hardly less distasteful now to some presbyterians than they are to episcopalians. Equally, presbyterians as well as episcopalians would now deplore the reformers' attempt to abolish the observance of the Christian Year; though it must be admitted that recent attempts at revival have not been conspicuously successful apart from Christmas and Easter, for outside church circles even Good Friday is thought of as no more than English Bank Holiday which has no relevance in Scotland. The reformers seem to have been apt to push perfectly sound principles just too far, in their anxiety to discard everything 'that ever flowed from that man of sin' [i.e., the Pope]. Thus, while there was a good deal to be said at the time for laying aside the eucharistic vestments, associated as they were with all the abuses which had grown up around the mass in later medieval times, it was a little severe to reject that simplest of all ecclesiastical garments, the surplice (especially as it was to be replaced by that much more elaborate, voluminous and expensive garment, the formidable pulpit gown).

However, there were cardinal points in the programme of the reformers which still command the allegiance of all the churches which adhere to the Reformation tradition: the open Bible in the language of the people; the participation in worship of congregations possessed of service-books and psalm-books in their own tongue; the rediscovery of the Communion as a corporate action; Communion in both kinds; clerical marriage; the participation of the laity in church affairs; the renewed emphasis on the parish; the revival of efficient oversight of clergy and churches; and—not least— the elimination of abuses. The Reformation, in the end, finds its justification in its fruits, for no church since the Reformation has ever again presented the picture of decay, of organized corruption, of persistent scandal, for which the unreformed church was notorious. Every church, including the Roman Catholic, is to that extent 'reformed'.

What the Reformation meant in the devotional life of the nation is reflected in some of the verses in the *Gude and godly ballates*.[1] It is true that their composition belongs to the earlier, Lutheran phase, before Calvinism became dominant in Scottish theology, but they were printed in 1567, 1578, 1600 and 1621, undoubtedly with official approval. The metrical version of the Apostles' Creed combines impeccable orthodoxy with vital faith:

'We trow in Jesus Christ his Sone,
God lyke in gloir, our Lord alone;
Quhilk, for his mercy and his grace,
Wald man be borne to mak our peace,
Of Mary mother Virgin chaist
Consavit be the Haly Gaist.
And for our saik on croce did die
Fra sin and hell to mak us fre:
And rais from deith, throw his Godheid,
Our Mediatour and our remeid,
Sall cum to Judge baith quick and deid.'

The verses on the Eucharist are 'catholic' in every sense of the word:

'And he, that we suld not foryet,
Gave us his body for to eit
In forme of breid, and gave us syne
His blude to drink in forme of wyne.

[1] Ed. David Laing, 1868.

Quha will ressave this Sacrament,
Suld have trew faith, and sin repent;
Quha usis it unworthelie,
Ressavis deid eternallie.

Thow suld not dout, bot fast beleve,
That Christis body sall releve
All them that ar in hevines
Repentand sair thair sinfulnes.'

When we read these lines we should recall the emphatic words in which the Scots Confession of Faith of 1560 declared its belief in a Real Presence:

'We utterly damn the vanity of those that affirm sacraments to be nothing else but naked and bare signs. . . . In the Supper, rightly used, Christ Jesus is so joined with us, that He becomes the very nourishment and food of our souls. . . . The faithful, in the right use of the Lord's Table, so do eat the body and drink the blood of the Lord Jesus, that He remaineth in them and they in Him.'

And there are remarkable stanzas which combine warm evangelical fervour with devotion to the Blessed Virgin:

'For us that blissit bairne was borne;
    For us he was baith rent and torne;
For us he was crownit with thorne;
    Christ hes my hart ay.

For us he sched his precious blude;
    For us he was naillit on the rude;
For us he in mony battell stude;
    Christ hes my hart ay.

Nixt him, to lufe his Mother fair,
    With steidfast hart, for ever mair;
Scho bure the byrth, fred us from cair;
    Christ hes my hart ay.'

This kind of thing transcends ecclesiastical bickerings. It speaks the same language as some of the medieval devotion referred to earlier, and shows how easily men of good will on the reforming side could have been reconciled with the moderate conservatives whose opinions are reflected in Archbishop Hamilton's Catechism.

6

THE RISE OF PRESBYTERIANISM

IT was not the intention of the reformers to divide the church, and they almost succeeded in preserving unity, for their programme, or at least their achievement, came near to securing the allegiance of the whole nation. There had been unanimity on the need for ecclesiastical reform, but, although it is not at all clear whether there was any practicable alternative to the course which events actually took, the proceedings of the reformers did not command universal support. Division into 'Protestants' or 'reformers' on one side and 'Catholics' or 'Roman Catholics' on the other, is an over-simplification, because until papal authority was reaffirmed, and Rome's doctrinal position defined, by the Council of Trent, there were many who defy such a classification. There were few in Scotland who put adherence to the papacy before all else, and the Archbishop of Glasgow, who might have rallied them, lost no time in making for the continent, never to return. There was much inarticulate and latent preference for the old ways and distaste for the new, but it is plain that the attachment to the church system which had been superseded was not comparable in strength to the attachment which presbytery and episcopacy in turn were to command in the following century. There was, indeed, a substantial body of opinion which might be called catholic but not Roman, generally conservative and traditionalist but ready for reform, possibly with some doctrinal modification although without revolutionary changes in church order. But there was hardly a middle *party*, and—partly because there seemed no prospect that this policy could be put into

effect and partly because the completion of the work of the
Council of Trent in 1563 presented a challenge which could
not be ignored—men of such views divided. Some decided
for Rome and joined the papalists on the continent, but others
passed into the reformed church, where they must have
exercised a moderating influence. The non-papal or national
catholic position had proved untenable. The consequence was
that organized opposition to the Reformation within Scotland was almost negligible, and the reformed church therefore almost succeeded in becoming the church of the nation.
Among those who supported the Reformation as it took
shape, and were within the reformed church from the outset,
some were probably more radical than others, and the more
moderate among them would be strengthened by the accession of the non-papal catholics. Yet, although (in Knox's
words) 'divers men were of divers judgments' in 1560 and it
is plain that there was a good deal of disagreement in theory,
as well as of diversity in liturgical practice, there is no indication of serious discord. The outbreak of strife within the
reformed church, and the creation of a situation which was
ultimately to lead to schism and secession, cannot be dated
either from 1560 or from 1572 (when the reformed church
took over the bishoprics).

It is to be dated from 1575, with the appearance of Andrew
Melville. As popular history is romantic history, Melville
has never been able to compete with Knox; the latter had
his interviews with Mary, Queen of Scots, while Melville
merely interviewed her less fascinating son, James VI (and
I)—whom he addressed as 'God's silly vassal'. The fact is,
however, that the John Knox of mythology is very largely
compounded of the Andrew Melville of history, for it was
Melville and not Knox who was the originator of Scottish
presbyterianism. Melville returned to Scotland in 1574, after
spending ten years at foreign universities, the last five of
those years at Geneva, where he absorbed the opinions of
Theodore Beza, whose teaching on the relations of church
and state and on ecclesiastical polity was more unyielding

than Calvin's. Unlike Knox, who had been a fiery preacher, pastoral and evangelical in his outlook, distrustful of the universities and often giving way to emotion, Melville was a scholar and a teacher, purely academic in his outlook and coldly rational in his thought. Melville never in his life served as a full-time parish minister and, with no experience of pastoral work, he could see no virtue in compromise or in concessions to expediency.

Melville's principles were directly at variance with those of the reformers. The equality, the parity, of the ministers of the Word and Sacraments must not be violated on any pretext whatever, and there must therefore be no bishops or superintendents. Neither should there be readers, even although there were not enough ministers for half the parishes in Scotland. The laity—whether as kings, estates, magistrates or annually elected elders—must be secluded from any voice in church affairs; instead, the church must have its own self-contained and exclusive polity, with a kirk session consisting of elders appointed for life,[1] presbyteries and synods consisting of ministers and elders and a General Assembly which no longer represented the estates of the realm but was likewise confined to ministers and elders. In his repudiation of lay control over the ministers and in his claim that the ministers, on their side, could 'teach the magistrate how to exercise the civil jurisdiction', Melville was reverting to a position which some have found it hard to distinguish from the medieval clericalism against which the reformation had revolted.

The contrast between Melville's views and those of the reformers, although it has been ignored or glossed over by many historians, was clear enough to contemporaries. Most of the older men, the men of Knox's generation, seem never to have become wholly favourable to Melville's schemes; and some of them opposed him, partly on the ground that episcopacy had scriptural sanction and partly on grounds of expediency, including the argument that as the Scots were

[1] Cf. p. 62 above.

an unruly people they could hardly, if at all, be retained in their duty unless constrained by the authority of bishops. But Melville, as a university principal, first at Glasgow and then at St Andrews, was in a commanding position, and formed a party of energetic, zealous and forthright young men who became for a time the most vigorous element in the church. In 1578 a presbyterian polity was approved by the General Assembly, in the second *Book of Discipline*. Melville and his followers then found that it was not enough to be victorious in the church, for the ecclesiastical constitution could not be changed except by statute law, and there followed a contest with the state. The government declined to recognize ecclesiastical independence and took up the Melvillian challenge by defining its standpoint in unmistakable terms in the so-called 'Black Acts' of 1584, which asserted the supremacy of the king in church affairs and virtually turned the bishops into crown commissioners for the administration of the church. At this point, therefore, if not earlier, two opposing points of view are clearly defined, for the supremacy of crown and parliament, and the episcopal office, stand on one side against the rule of the General Assembly, and ministerial parity, on the other.

The great controversy between those two points of view was not merely a matter of Scottish history; it was a matter of British history. Ever since the Reformation, indeed, Anglo-Scottish ecclesiastical affairs had been intermingled. The Scottish reformers were not only anglophile in their politics, but had come under strong English influence; John Knox had lived so long in England and among Englishmen and Englishwomen (one of whom he married) that he acquired an English accent—a fact which his enemies never allowed him to forget. The Reformation gave Scotland a Bible, service-books and a Psalter in the English tongue, and was a strong factor in the assimilation of Scottish speech to that of England. From 1560 there had never been wanting those who looked to 'conformity' to cement the 'amity' between the two countries, and the claim of Queen Mary

Notre Dame College
of Education
BEARSDEN, GLASGOW
LIBRARY

and James VI to be the heirs of the unmarried Elizabeth opened up the prospect of a union between the two countries which contemporaries considered to be unthinkable unless it should be accompanied by ecclesiastical uniformity. 'Conformity' between England and Scotland, or something like it, was being achieved, on an episcopalian basis, in 1572. But in that very year the presbyterian programme was enunciated in England by Thomas Cartwright, who, like Melville, had been in Geneva. Not only were the English and Scottish presbyterian movements parallel, but they were closely associated, and in 1580 Cartwright and Travers (who, in Fuller's words, were the 'head' and 'neck' of English presbyterianism) were invited to chairs at St Andrews university, where Melville was principal. Cartwright and Melville were as eager for 'conformity' between the realms as their opponents, but conformity on their basis, the presbyterian-puritan basis, was never to be attained, and the effect of their work was in the end to bring about that conspicuous lack of conformity which was to persist from 1690 until the present.

In both kingdoms the presbyterian movements represented a serious threat to the existing church order, and even in England the issue was for a time in doubt. The reason why the outcome was so different in the two countries was certainly, at least in part, political. Queen Elizabeth was not only personally resolute to maintain episcopacy and the Prayer Book, but she had at her command a stable and effective governmental machine and—in spite of her personal preference for a modest ritual which shocked the churchmen of the time as well as the puritans—both she and her governments were indubitably Protestant. In Scotland, by contrast, there was a royal minority followed by some periods of ineffective rule; and a government which was more than once suspected of being too tender to the papalist cause antagonised Protestant feeling and found it impossible to avert the temporary triumph of presbyterianism. King James was for a long time irresolute, in his public professions if not in his own mind, and his ultimate resolution was not matched by the necessary authority until long after the Presbyterians had won substantial successes, the memory of which could never be obliterated. It should be added that Queen Elizabeth, who never seems to have thought of Anglicanism as a commodity for export, repeatedly declined to support Scottish governments which would have maintained episcopacy, and instead used Scottish Presbyterians as her agents. To that extent she must bear part of the responsibility for the triumph of Andrew Melville.

The whole period of the controversy between the presbyterian and episcopalian parties in the Church of Scotland, from 1575 to 1690, has the appearance of alternating phases of one system of church order and the other—episcopacy in 1584, presbytery in 1592, episcopacy in 1610, presbytery in 1638, episcopacy in 1661 and presbytery in 1690. And it is a notable truth that the Church of Scotland then comprehended two opposing parties, of which now one, now the other, attained a temporary ascendancy. Unity of opinion had been disrupted, for there were two parties, but the unity of the church was still maintained, for the two parties remained within it. It was all a little like parliamentary government, in which two parties alternately achieve power and the party which is for the time being out of power, instead of seceding and declaring itself a rival parliament, remains within the one parliament, awaiting the time when it will be in the ascendant once more. So it was in the Scottish church. The party which was for the time being out of office, as it were, did not go into schism and form a rival communion, but remained within the church, working for the restoration of the church order which it believed to be the better one. The idea of unity was still so strong that men submitted to much of which they did not approve rather than abandon the national church.

In this situation, sometimes every parish church in Scotland was an episcopalian church, sometimes every parish church in Scotland was a presbyterian church. But never

was there an episcopalian parish church under a presbyterian regime, or—except in the last two or three years before
1690—a presbyterian parish church under an episcopalian
regime. This may seem elementary and obvious, but it is a
necessary corrective to some absurd statements which sometimes appear in print. There seems to be an idea that in some
mystic manner the Scottish church remained presbyterian
even when it was governed by bishops. For instance, it has
been stated that in 1572, after the General Assembly, the
Privy Council and the Parliament had approved of bishops,
'the church, established by law, remained presbyterian'[1]—
which in fact it had never yet been. Again, the account of
Robert Baillie in the *Dictionary of National Biography* states
that about 1622 he 'received orders not from the Church of
Scotland—i.e. Presbyterians—but from Archbishop Law of
Glasgow' and goes on to note with surprise that 'in spite of
his episcopal ordination' he was presented to a parish in the
Church of Scotland. And a prominent historian, speaking of
the incumbent of a parish in Charles II's reign—an incumbent
who had been ordained and admitted by a bishop—said 'Of
course he was a presbyterian minister.' Such statements
disclose a wilful refusal to accept facts.

Yet while these are truths, and important truths, to think
of the polity of the church as oscillating from one extreme
to the other, between a complete presbyterian system and a
complete episcopal system, is misleading. Time and again what
was being tried was essentially a compromise which would
satisfy the theories of the Presbyterians but at the same
time leave room in practice for an episcopate of a kind and
for a measure of royal or parliamentary control over the
church. Right at the outset, in 1575, and again in 1586, there
were attempts to find a formula which would accommodate
the theoretical parity of all ministers and the equation of the
bishop with the minister of the parish but at the same time
provide for a working constitutional episcopacy not unlike
that of the 'bishop-in-presbytery' which has been proposed

[1] Gillon, *John Davidson*, 1935, p. 56.

again in modern schemes. It was admitted that all ministers were bishops, but some of them received special commissions to act as administrators: in short, it was suggested, all ministers are bishops but some are more bishops than others.

In 1592 Parliament did for the first time approve a presbyterian system, but did not surrender to Melville. The statute did not proceed on any allusion to the divine right of the presbyterian system, neither did it concede ecclesiastical independence. The crown had the right to name the time and place of the General Assembly's meetings and, although it was stated that an Assembly should normally meet each year, no machinery was provided to ensure that one would meet if the crown declined to summon it. Synods and presbyteries likewise received recognition, and presbyteries were in operation throughout most of the country, but individual overseers—'visitors' and 'commissioners'—continued to play an important part in administration. Besides, the office of bishop, though certainly eclipsed, was not abolished, and 'bishops' of a kind there still were (as well as 'archdeacons', 'deans' and so forth). In the kirk sessions, the practice of annual election of elders was still usual, and a long time was yet to pass before the principle 'Once an elder, always an elder' was generally accepted. The General Assembly was not transformed into the gathering of ministers and elders envisaged by Melville, for 'barons' and representatives of burghs still took their places. Finally, while no specific provision was made for the representation of a presbyterian church in Parliament, the general assumption was that clerical representation of some kind was to continue.

This makeshift system was such that an administrative episcopate could be reintroduced without causing any serious dislocation, and the fact that the method of representation in Parliament had not been defined invited an arrangement whereby ministers should be appointed to vacant bishoprics to qualify them to sit as part of the spiritual estate. King James used both those approaches to a restoration of episcopacy and further strengthened his bishops by reverting to a feature of the compromise proposed in 1586 and having them acknowledged as permanent presidents—'constant moderators'—of presbyteries and synods. By so arranging meetings of the General Assembly as to facilitate the attendance of ministers from north of the Tay, where opinion was less radical than in the south, and by recourse to bribery, intimidation and trickery, he obtained approval of his proceedings. In 1610, the administrative episcopate which James had built up received a sanction which neither king nor assembly could confer on it, for three Scottish bishops then received consecration in England, but although the normal succession was thus restored and although there are indications, even before this, that the reformers' denial of succession was being discarded, there was no question of asking men in presbyterian orders to accept episcopal ordination. The Jacobean episcopate was not fatal to the General Assembly, which remained the highest authority in the church, and might be manipulated but could not be ignored; and so far from episcopacy being detrimental to the rest of the presbyterian system, all the indications are that the association of bishops with presbyteries and synods worked smoothly and that under their joint direction the parish ministry and the discipline of the kirk session operated better than before. Not only so, but it was in this period and no earlier that adequate financial resources were at last put at the disposal of the reformed church, and this made possible the expansion of the ministry throughout the country, the provision of many parish schools and the erection and improvement of church buildings, so that many of the schemes of John Knox received their fulfilment under this episcopal regime. The initiation of the compromise between presbytery and episcopacy had arisen mainly from practical, or at least non-theological, considerations, and those who worked it out may not have had the deliberate intention of combining the merits of the two systems, but that result was undoubtedly achieved.

In early seventeenth-century Scotland, then, we find the

bishop-in-presbytery, we find the introduction of an episcopate, impeccably consecrated, without the reordination of
men in presbyterian orders, we find recognition accorded
by the Church of England to a church with a ministry not
entirely episcopally ordained, a church which did not have
'the threefold ministry' as Anglicans understand it, a church
where confirmation by a bishop was unknown. Presbytery
and episcopacy may be based on irreconcilable principles,
but if it is possible to achieve a working compromise between
the two, such a compromise was achieved in that period.
And there have been many since, both Presbyterians and
Episcopalians, who have regretted that this compromise did
not endure. Scotland, which has been such an example of
disunity, narrowly missed becoming a model of unity.

The moderate episcopalian regime of the early seventeenth century proved generally acceptable to the Scots.
While a few ministers continued to advocate the views of
Melville, the majority, of clergy and laity alike, acquiesced.
The ordinary layman, of course, saw relatively little change
at local level when polity was modified. Whether ultimate
power lies with a General Assembly or an episcopal synod
makes little difference in the day-to-day life of a congregation. And in the seventeenth century the impact of the bishop
on the congregation must have been even less marked than
it is today, partly because Scottish dioceses contained far
more parishes then than now, partly because of difficulty of
communication, and partly because the presbytery, in one
form or another, stood between the bishop and the congregation. And if the ordinary layman was thus conscious of little
change in organization, he was also conscious, for some time
at least, of no changes whatsoever in worship. It was only
when changes in worship were made that opposition was
aroused among the laity and the whole fabric of the Jacobean
compromise endangered.

7

THE REJECTION OF EPISCOPACY

THE essential controversy had hitherto been, and in the main it continued to be, a controversy over church order and not over either doctrine or forms of worship. The disputes in recent years over proposals to revive the office of bishop in the Church of Scotland have done something to focus attention once more on the matter really at issue, but to many people in Scotland today 'Episcopacy' is still apt to suggest primarily a Prayer Book, an altar and a surplice, while 'Presbytery' connotes a sermon, a pulpit and a black gown. In the seventeenth century, both parties at first accepted as their doctrinal standard the Scots Confession of 1560, but even after the Presbyterians, in circumstances which we shall examine later, adopted a new, English Confession (the Westminster Confession) there were few signs of any tendency to set one theology against another. So it was, throughout most of this period, with forms of worship. The Scottish church could be episcopalian in its order without a compulsory Prayer Book, without a surplice, without altarwise worship or kneeling at Communion.

The Scottish reformers had begun by using the English Prayer Book. They were not in favour of everything that book contained, but then neither were most of their English contemporaries. In Scotland, however, where there was no 'godly prince' (or princess) as supreme governor, able to defend the Prayer Book as Queen Elizabeth defended it, the demand for something more radical was unchecked. Therefore the Scots turned readily to another English servicebook, the Book of Common Order, which had been compiled for English exiles on the continent during Mary Tudor's reign. The Prayer Book was not thereby wholly displaced, for some still preferred it, and in any event the Book of Common Order—'Knox's Liturgy'—was no mere directory, for prayers were undoubtedly read from the book and the 'reading of prayers' was a regular part of public worship. Besides, the Lord's Prayer, the Apostles' Creed and the Doxology were all in use and there were metrical versions of the Nunc Dimittis and of 'the song of Blessed Marie, called Magnificat'.

From about 1600, if not earlier, the opinion was widespread, not only among men of episcopalian views, that the liturgy required enrichment and that there should be more uniformity in worship. On this foundation, the project of a revised service-book was taken up by the king and the General Assembly, and for a time there were very good prospects that a revision representing a compromise between the Book of Common Order and the Book of Common Prayer might be generally acceptable to the Scots. But the king complicated the issue when, concurrently with the liturgical projects, he put forward requirements which came to be known as the Five Articles of Perth. At least two of those articles—the observance of the principal holy days in the Christian year and the permissive administration of baptism privately—were supported by a good deal of popular opinion and indeed were in accord with some current practice. Two further articles—private administration of Communion and the examination of children by bishops on their visitations—were not gravely controversial and did not affect ordinary worship. But the fifth article, to the effect that communicants should kneel to receive the Sacrament, was something which touched every worshipper, and the Scots, although they were then accustomed to kneel for prayer, had scruples lest kneeling at Communion should imply adoration of an objective Real Presence in the elements. This article consequently aroused opposition far more widespread than any which had been occasioned by disputes over

F

polity. The king did not withdraw, but he agreed to make
no further changes as long as he lived, the bishops did not
press the Articles, the project of liturgical revision was laid
aside, and when James died in 1625 he left a church in which
there was little overt unrest.

Charles I, who succeeded him, lacked his father's subtlety
as well as his father's understanding of the Scottish tempera-
ment, and in a dozen years he had alienated almost every
section of his Scottish subjects. The nobility found that the
security of their tenure of church property which they had
acquired before or since the Reformation was now threatened;
nobles, officials and lawyers were jealous of the bishops,
whom Charles advanced to high offices in the state; all who
cared for their constitutional rights were alienated by the
king's manipulation of Parliament; and heavy taxation aroused
discontent in the burghs, and especially in the capital, Edinburgh. When Charles in 1629 revived the project of a new
Prayer Book for Scotland, the Scottish bishops were emphatic that Scotland must be provided with a liturgy distinct
from that of England, while the king's English advisers
wanted to see the English book, without any change, imposed in Scotland. Charles attempted to compromise by
instructing the Scots, in 1634, to revise the English book
within certain limits and subject to review by himself and
his English advisers. Of the book which emerged it is now
possible to assert with confidence that its principal characteristics, especially in the Communion Office, were the work
of Scottish bishops, and that Archbishop Laud, by whose
name it is known, had very little to do with it. It authorized
some existing Scottish practices, such as the inclusion in the
Communion Office of an *epiklesis*, or invocation of the Holy
Spirit on the elements, and it made concessions to Scottish
prejudice, as in the use of the term 'presbyter' instead of
'priest'. On the other hand, it permitted the presbyter, when
consecrating the elements at Communion, to stand in front
of the Holy Table, with his back to the people, which at once
recalled the mass, and the king personally insisted on the

retention or introduction of other features which were bound to be unpopular in Scotland—a proclamation making it clear that the book was being imposed by the royal prerogative, the inclusion in the table of lessons of twelve chapters from the Apocrypha (which had been disused in Scottish worship since the Reformation) and a Kalendar with more saints' days and festivals than the contemporary English book had.

It may be doubted whether any new liturgy could have been considered on its merits, because the country was seething with discontent over its many secular grievances. The reading of the new liturgy for the first time in the cathedral of St Giles in Edinburgh on 23 July 1637 was the occasion, but not the cause, of the revolt which was to bring down Charles's government. The introduction of the Prayer Book was the opportunity for a demonstration which would appeal to the popular feeling against popery, against English interference in Scottish affairs, and against arbitrary rule, and it led to rioting and widespread supplications against the 'innovations' in worship.

Seven months after the riot of 23 July came the National Covenant. The many people who refer to this document without ever having read it often say that it condemned episcopal government. It did no such thing, and indeed went to some pains to avoid doing so. What it did say was that the signatories would 'forbear the practice of all novations already introduced in the matters of the worship of God, or approbation of the corruptions of the public government of the kirk, or civil places and power of kirkmen, till they be tried and allowed in free assemblies and in parliaments'. This was modest enough, and the whole tenor of the Covenant is that of an appeal to the law and constitution against proceedings by the king which were deemed illegal. It is, in truth, a somewhat tedious document, beginning with the recital of an old anti-popish covenant of 1581 and half of the remainder consisting of a list of statutes which the king was held to have infringed. It was carefully framed to appeal to all who had grievances against the king's policies.

The reason why the Covenant captured the imagination and won the devoted zeal of so many Scots was that it flattered their national conceit. The idea that the Scots were a specially favoured people, and even a Chosen People, goes back to the St Andrew legends and is explicit in the Declaration of Arbroath,[1] and it had been reinforced by their belief in the unique purity of their reformed church. Knox, after explaining carefully the traces of papistry in other churches, added: 'we, all praise to God alone, have nothing within our churches that ever flowed from that Man of Sin.' Now, with the Covenant, Scotland was the new Israel, the bride of Christ, who, it was claimed, 'will embrace both us, the little young sister, and the Church of the Jews.' It escaped notice that this imputed incestuous bigamy to the Almighty.

The condemnation of episcopacy came after the Covenant, and this was only natural, for not only had a presbyterian system never yet been in full operation, but a generation had now grown to maturity under a form of church government in which bishops had had a part. Contemporary accounts make it clear not only that the critics of the Prayer Book were extremely reluctant to proceed to a condemnation of episcopacy, but also that it was simply not generally known that the office of bishop had ever been condemned. Episcopal government was not abolished until the Glasgow Assembly in November 1638, nine months after the Covenant had been signed, and even then there were long debates before a decision was reached that episcopacy should be not only 'removed' but also 'abjured'. It is quite plain that the attack on episcopacy was only a secondary development in a revolt which had broken out over quite different issues.

It was not only in this matter of church order that the Covenanters went further than the Covenant. Although pledged in the Covenant to the defence of the king, they intervened in England after the civil war started, making common cause with the English parliamentarians and entering into an alliance with them in the Solemn League and

[1] p. 28 above.

Covenant (1643), which envisaged the creation of a British church on the presbyterian-puritan model. No one on the episcopalian side in Scotland had as yet gone so far as to advocate complete Anglo-Scottish uniformity on an English model, but now the standards of worship for the whole of Britain were to be those of the English puritans. The concept of 'unity without uniformity', dear to some modern Presbyterians, had no appeal in the seventeenth century. The Covenanters, not content with rejecting recent innovations (as the Covenant pledged them to do), now rejected all prescribed prayers and all 'set forms'. The Creed, the Lord's Prayer and the Commandments, though they had been retained by John Knox, came to be characterized as 'old rotten wheelbarrows to carry souls to hell'. It was at this period, and not at the Reformation, that the characteristics of Scottish presbyterian worship originated. The forms of worship (and also the formulae relating to doctrine and government) which the Covenanters adopted and to which the presbyterian Church of Scotland still adheres were drawn up by an assembly of divines at Westminster, where English representatives numbered over a hundred and only eight Scots were present as 'assistants'. It is a little curious that the Confession of Faith of Scottish Presbyterians, their Larger and Shorter Catechisms, their Directory of Public Worship and their Form of Church Government are all plainly marked on their title-pages 'Made in England'. And it has been observed that the presbyterian gibe that it was unpatriotic of Scottish bishops to seek consecration at Westminster is a little inappropriate.

With this covenanting period of the 1640s a new bitterness entered into Scottish church affairs. The Reformation had been conducted with remarkable mildness, and since the Reformation the bitterest critics of the bishops never accused them of being persecutors. But now, under the covenanting regime, divisions arose compared to which the presbyterian-episcopalian controversy had been mere friendly rivalry. The divisions were between different shades of

Presbyterians—between those who opposed, and those who favoured, intervention in the English civil war; between those who stood by the king and those who were ready to abandon him to his fate; between those who put the national cause first (when Scotland was threatened by Oliver Cromwell) and those who would let no one fight for his country unless his ecclesiastical politics were sound; and between those who conceded that the people of England might have some say in the choice of a form of government for their own church and those who insisted that presbyterianism must be imposed on the whole of the British Isles. When the most extreme and unyielding faction prevailed, the church dominated national policy and possessed a veto on all public appointments, whether in central government, local government or armed forces. There was not only the 'purge' from office of those who would not toe the party line, but there was also much 'liquidation': with the blood-chilling cry, 'Jesus and no quarter!' the Covenanters massacred not only prisoners who had surrendered on conditions but even the women and children who followed their enemies' camp. The covenanting movement, which had started as a nation-wide protest against the arbitrary rule of a king, degenerated into an attempt to impose a new tyranny, and to impose it in England and Ireland as well. It is an elementary error to believe that the Covenanters were ever interested in 'freedom', or 'liberty', as we understand these terms. They claimed freedom for themselves; but they would concede no freedom to others. One who had written in 1637 (when he was in opposition), 'Who can blame us for standing to the defence of our Christian liberty?' wrote eight years later (when his party was in power), 'Liberty of conscience ought not to be granted.'[1] Still less were the Covenanters interested in toleration, which was denounced as 'wicked' and as contrary to the Covenants (which it was). When Scotland did fall under the sway of the government of Oliver Cromwell,

[1] George Gillespie, *English Popish ceremonies* (1637), p. 4; *Sermon preached before the House of Lords, 27 August, 1645*, p. 14.

which imposed toleration (though not for episcopalians and papists), the General Assembly was sent packing, in 1653.

When Charles II was restored to his father's throne in 1660, the existing 'beheaded' presbyterian system, with kirk sessions, synods and presbyteries, was preserved, but Cromwell's work in dispensing with the General Assembly was not undone, and instead bishops were reinstated; however, because of a strong anti-clerical reaction—the consequence of the domination of politics by the covenanting ministers in the 1640s—the church was subjected very firmly to king, council and Parliament, and the bishops had no freedom to frame policy. The revival of episcopacy was made once more without challenging presbyterian orders. Bishops did persuade a number of Presbyterians to receive episcopal ordination, and some Presbyterians sought it voluntarily; but the bishops do not seem to have used any compulsion and it was formally recognized that men could have 'entered the holy ministry' by presbyterial ordination. This renewed experiment in compromise on an episcopalian basis has been less highly thought of than the Jacobean experiment, but it is equally worthy of examination. The episcopate conformed to the Anglican pattern in little save the civil position of the bishops as one of the estates of the realm and, of course, their sole right to ordain (though it is far from clear if the 'plain and Protestant' forms used in ordination were such as would be acceptable by modern Anglican standards).[1] Legislative power and appellate jurisdiction lay with the bishop-in-synod, executive authority very largely with the presbyteries, which were mainly responsible for the visitation of churches and the examination of candidates for ordination. Further, presbyteries sometimes voluntarily submitted difficult cases to the bishop and asked his advice, and authority seems to have been shared with hardly any friction. Although a bishop might preside over the kirk session and

[1] It has been suggested that Scottish episcopalian orders in consequence remained defective until the late nineteenth century (T. F. Taylor, *A profest papist: Bishop John Gordon*, 1959, pp. 5, 11).

the presbytery which met in his cathedral city, these courts in general carried on their functions with a good deal of independence. Confirmation by the bishop was unknown and the ordination of ministerial deacons extremely rare. The worship of the church differed little from that which had developed in covenanting times, though there were signs of an attempt to revert to the forms which had prevailed between the Reformation and the seventeenth-century movements which had sought to re-shape Scottish worship into conformity with English standards, first on an Anglican and later on a puritan model. The whole of church life reflects a serious attempt to work out a native solution, without slavish imitation of England or anywhere else.

But the bitterness born of the strife which had followed the Covenants had left its mark. The divisions among the Covenanters were not to be healed, so there could have been no settlement by consent, no settlement universally acceptable, and probably no settlement which would have resulted in any less discontent than did the settlement actually adopted. The more moderate party, called 'Resolutioners', generally took the view that a moderate episcopalian regime offered the best chance of peace and unity, but the extremists, or 'Protesters', adhering to the Covenants as eternally binding, were bound to reject anything less than the policy of the presbyterian crusade for the subjection of the British Isles. Therefore in the Restoration period there were for the first time those who declined to worship in the parish churches and instead met in conventicles. They rejected the parish churches not because the form of service there differed from their own, but because the established church had bishops and had laid aside the Covenants. These conventiclers were concerned for the Melvillian ideal of ecclesiastical independence, or the liberation of the church from control by king, council and Parliament, and the extremists among them, the Cameronians, ultimately renounced their allegiance to King Charles. But they were not interested in 'freedom', in the sense of toleration, or in democracy, which they characterized as government 'after a carnal manner, by plurality of votes'. The myth of this period is that the Scots were a nation of Presbyterians and that everywhere the people refused to worship in the parish churches under ministers who accepted the rule of bishops, and instead met in conventicles, where they had 'freedom to worship God in their own way'. But—apart from the fact that how people worshipped God was not the issue—the episcopal regime was widely acceptable. The conventicle movement, very strong in the south-west, was weaker elsewhere and in many large areas non-existent.

The government tried to deal with the opposition partly by coercion. It is very doubtful if as much blood was shed by the Restoration government as had been shed by the Covenanters during their ascendancy in the 1640s.[1] Moreover, those who were killed in encounters with government troops, or executed, in the Restoration period, suffered not because they were Presbyterians but because they were rebels, not because they renounced bishops but because they took up arms against the king. But it is one of those points in history where facts cannot prevail against folk-memory. 'It is news to me,' remarked one Presbyterian Scot in 1957, 'that the Covenanters massacred women and children. I refuse to believe it!' The martyrology of the 'Killing Time', on the other hand, suitably publicized generation by generation and kept alive by commemorative 'conventicles', still does much to shape Scottish opinion on the subject of bishops. But there were phases of concession as well as of coercion, and one feature of the policy of concession was the 'indulgence', which meant that ministers of presbyterian views could serve parishes without taking any part in church government—a remarkable indication of a belief that the national church could comprehend men of radically different opinions. Partly by concession, partly by repression, the strength of the conventicle movement was gradually worn

[1] For an inscription suitable for a 'Martyrs' Monument' to commemorate the victims of the Covenanters, see M. E. M. Donaldson, *Scotland's suppressed history*, 1935, pp. 82–4.

down and the opposition was divided within itself. It is hard to escape the conclusion that in time the church would have settled down permanently under this moderate episcopalian regime and that once more there would have been a united church and a united people.

That this did not happen was due to a new and extraneous factor, the Roman Catholic policy of James VII, who succeeded his brother, Charles II, in 1685. James first requested concessions for his co-religionists from the Scottish Parliament, which refused to comply, and he then proceeded to grant a toleration which he extended not only to Roman Catholics but to all his subjects, including the Presbyterians. It would have been plain to anyone less obtuse than James that however effective the royal authority might be, and however strong the attachment to the dynasty, concessions to papists would arouse the greatest repugnance. But James, with his unerring instinct for doing the wrong thing, had chosen to raise the one issue which would bring down his throne. It is a striking commentary on the attachment to religious liberty with which seventeenth-century Scots are too often credited that when toleration came it was the most unpopular measure of the century. Nothing was so intolerable as toleration. But that was not all. Three generations of the house of Stewart had endeavoured to weld the Scottish nation into ecclesiastical unity on a moderate episcopalian foundation. Success had hardly ever been nearer, when James at one stroke undid the work of a century.

It had never been possible, under Charles II, to raise more than a small minority of the Scottish people to arms on the cry of 'No prelacy'. But now there was a nation-wide revulsion against the king on the cry of 'No popery'. The Scots might not, indeed, have attempted a revolution independently, but James's unpopularity in England led to his flight and his replacement in that country by William of Orange, the husband of his daughter, Mary. A convention of estates, with the same membership as a parliament, thereupon met in Edinburgh. It was far from unanimous, but after the withdrawal of the supporters of James (who were presumably all Episcopalians), the remainder drew up a declaration asserting that James had forfeited the crown and offering it to William and Mary, and the Presbyterians secured the insertion in this declaration of a resolution that 'prelacy, and the superiority of any office in the church above presbyters, is and hath been a great and insupportable grievance and trouble to this nation, ever since the Reformation, and therefore ought to be abolished.' This was not decisive, but the Scottish bishops themselves went far to ensure their downfall. They had recently addressed James as the darling of heaven, and the Bishop of Edinburgh, sent to represent them in London, learned to his dismay that the darling of heaven had fled to France and the Prince of Orange was in Whitehall. He found William not unfriendly, and disposed to maintain episcopacy in Scotland, but the bishop declined to commit himself to support the new king: 'Sir, I shall serve you as far as law, reason and conscience will allow.'[1] William and Mary were accepted as king and queen of Scots in April 1689, but the Scottish bishops were to a man loyal to James. This did not in itself settle their fate. However, the Presbyterians had taken advantage of the toleration granted by James to build up their organization into something like an alternative to the establishment; in the south-west the episcopalian clergy were driven out by the mob; in other parts of the country clergy were in trouble for declining to pray for William and Mary; and the convention, by withholding taxation, put pressure on the king to comply with its wishes. Ultimately, in 1690, William gave way, and agreed to a statute restoring the presbyterian system.

Thus episcopacy was rejected a second time, but again its rejection had been a secondary development in a movement which had started over a different issue—this time the popish policy of James VII. It is true that in 1689 there was

[1] The bishop's account of the negotiations is in Robert Keith, *Scottish Bishops*, 1824, pp. 65 ff., and F. Goldie. *A short history of the Episcopal Church in Scotland*, 1951, pp. 151 ff.

an active presbyterian party, as there had not been in 1637, but once more episcopal government was rejected because of its association with something else. But for the incurable Jacobitism of the bishops in 1689, presbyterianism might never have been established again.

The settlement of 1690 was a more complete settlement, and a more thoroughly presbyterian settlement, than that of 1592 had been. The office of bishop, name and thing, was formally abolished, and the door by which episcopacy had been re-insinuated a century earlier was firmly closed, at the cost of relinquishing clerical representation in Parliament. Yet the settlement was not a victory for the theories of Andrew Melville, and still less a victory for the upholders of the Covenants, whose views were simply dismissed. There was no recognition of ecclesiastical independence: the presbyterian system was set up not by any ecclesiastical organ, nor through any abdication of function on the part of Parliament; it was set up by Parliament, in the same way as previous presbyterian and episcopalian constitutions. It was set up not on the grounds of any superior claim to divine right, but on the purely secular ground that it was pronounced to be agreeable to the inclinations of the generality of the people. The civil penalties which had previously attached to excommunication, and the duties of the magistrate to support the censures of the kirk, were abrogated. It was abundantly demonstrated in succeeding years that the church was still subject to Parliament, and contemporaries were in no doubt that what one Parliament had conceded another Parliament could withdraw. The establishment of presbyterianism was further tied to statute law in 1707, when the Parliaments of England and Scotland were united, for it was then declared to be a 'fundamental and essential' condition of the union that the existing government of the Church of Scotland should be maintained. The idea that the Church of Scotland in some way gained its 'freedom' in 1690 is quite without foundation. Independence of England it had gained so long ago as 1192, independence of Crown and

Parliament it was not to gain until 1921.[1]

No steps were taken to ascertain the views of the 'generality of the people' upon which the new establishment professed to be founded, and from that time to this there has been controversy as to the relative strength of the episcopalian and presbyterian parties. The great majority of the parish clergy were episcopalian, since episcopacy had been established for a generation, and this fact made it impracticable for ecclesiastical polity to be the subject of discussion in a genuinely representative General Assembly, for such an Assembly, with its episcopalian majority, would at once have swept away the new establishment. It is equally true that most congregations found their ministers acceptable and wanted to retain them—not because of their ideas of the rights and wrongs of bishops and presbyters, but simply out of personal attachment. It is true, further, that the enthusiastic presbyterianism of the south-west was counterbalanced by an equally genuine affection for episcopacy in the north-east. Beyond that it is dangerous to go, though it may be noted that while some Presbyterians have conceded that the Episcopalians were the more numerous party, no Episcopalian has ever conceded the contrary; and it may be further observed that among the clergy there was a far larger majority for episcopacy now, after twenty-eight years of episcopalian rule, than there had been for presbytery in 1661 after twenty-three years of presbyterian rule.[2]

However, the state of opinion did little to shape the course of events. The presbyterian strength grew rapidly, with the support of the law and the government, while the Episcopalians, deprived of the buttress of establishment, were too bewildered to offer much resistance, and as rapidly dwindled. The bishops saw the solution of their difficulties only in a restoration of King James, and could not bring themselves to believe that William's triumph was anything but transient.

[1] See p. 101 below.
[2] Less than 300 clergy had to be deprived after the Restoration; more than 500 were deprived after the Revolution.

The old situation of two parties within one church, and the old unity of church and nation, came to an end with the eviction of the Episcopalians from the establishment. There were now in practice two churches in Scotland; but the law did not yet acknowledge the fact, for there was no toleration. Indeed it may be said that the one survival after 1690 of the old concept of unity, the ideal of the comprehension of all Scots within one church, was the unhappy one that attempts at coercion continued. When a measure of toleration was conceded to Episcopalians in 1712, it came from the British Parliament and in the teeth of bitter opposition from the General Assembly. If continued attempts at coercion were the sole survival of the policy of comprehension, all other tendencies were in the other direction, and the floodgates of schism and secession opened up with a vengeance.

8

PRESBYTERIAN DIVISIONS
AND REUNIONS

IT was in the 1690s that there began to take shape something like the modern situation, in which several communions compete for the allegiance of Scotsmen. Not
only does the presbyterian-episcopalian schism date from
this point; and not only, as we shall see later, was it in this
period that the sustained and consistent Roman Catholic
effort began; but it was then that the presbyterian body itself
began that process of fragmentation which was to be a conspicuous feature of the next century and a half. Division had
now gone so deep that no amount of tinkering with the
established ecclesiastical system could any longer avail to
preserve even external unity, as it had in the main succeeded
in doing hitherto; moreover, the new establishment of 1690
was at first hopelessly under-manned, so that large areas of
the country were driven to accept any ministrations which
might be offered; and further, the very virtues of the 1690
via media meant that if it could not satisfy the Episcopalians
neither could it satisfy the more radical Presbyterians. The
Cameronians, who adhered strictly to the Covenants, repudiated the new uncovenanted establishment as they had
repudiated the old, and remained outside it, to form later the
Reformed Presbyterian Church, which—although a large
part of it joined the Free Church in 1876—still exists, persist-
ing in its refusal to acknowledge an uncovenanted government. Besides, the large central body comprehended in the
new establishment was too heterogeneous to hold together

for long. There were those within it who regretted that the Covenants had been laid aside and wanted to re-impose on the state the duty to support the censures of the church; there were those who inclined to a rigid Calvinist theology; there were those who found parliamentary control irksome and revived claims to ecclesiastical independence. On the other hand, there were those of liberal, sometimes of almost rationalist, theology, whom their opponents accused of abandoning theology altogether and preaching mere ethics. Divisions might therefore have come about even had the connection with the state not from time to time imposed a considerable strain and even had the rights of individual lay patrons not been restored by Parliament in 1712. Patronage was no innovation, for it had existed during nearly all the period since the Reformation until abolished in 1690, but its restoration was likely to cause trouble within a church already divided, since patron and congregation might have different theological views.

The second group to secede—if we count the Cameronians as the first—were the Glassites, who, about 1730, reacted against the whole idea of an established church and a professional ministry, and made a remarkable attempt to return to the most primitive Christian practice. They never became a large body, but still maintain a tenuous existence.

The so-called First or Original Secession, in 1733, arose out of the various disturbing factors already at work, and represented a reaction towards a conservative theology and adherence to the Covenants; far from repudiating the state connection in theory, it stressed the duty of the state to maintain the church—though of course under the direction of the church. This body divided, first because some scrupled to take an oath in which burgesses had to acknowledge 'the true religion presently professed', and secondly over the question of the duties in matters of religion ascribed to the civil magistrate by the Westminster Confession of Faith, so that by the first decade of the nineteenth century the First Secession consisted of Old Light Burghers, New Light

Burghers, Old Light Anti-Burghers and New Light Anti-Burghers.

The Second Secession, or Relief Church, founded in 1761, arose directly from disputes over patronage, and soon came to stand for the 'voluntary' principle, or the principle that the church should not seek establishment or maintenance from the state.

With the exception of the Glassites and the Relief Church, the secessions had all been backward-looking, in reaction against the liberal tendencies in the establishment, which during the greater part of the eighteenth century was moving with the times and assimilating a good deal of the changing thought of the age. The 'moderatism' which prevailed in the Church of Scotland in this period is analogous to the contemporary latitudinarianism of the Church of England; for the moderates, tolerant and 'enlightened', determined to show that Charles II had been wrong when he said that presbyterianism was no religion for gentlemen, were distrustful of 'enthusiasm'. It would, however, be an error to regard the Scottish secessions as parallel to English Methodism, for the affinities between them were swallowed up in differences of theology and ecclesiastical politics. Later in the eighteenth century a new liberalism arose; it showed itself in politics in demands for the extension of the franchise and in more radical movements associated with the French Revolution, and it showed itself in religion in a humanitarian and evangelical solicitude for the churchless masses in the growing industrial towns and for the heathen overseas. For such generous impulses the establishment seemed to have little room. The moderate majority in the General Assembly (while not repudiating the obligation to propagate Christianity overseas) refused in 1796 to countenance the recently formed inter-denominational foreign mission societies, and it was the liberal or evangelical party who raised the money for 'church extension' and who developed Sunday schools.

One result of this situation was the appearance of a good deal of evangelical work outside the existing church system,

G

not only in towns but also in some of the most remote parts of the country, where the establishment was clearly failing to provide a vigorous enough spiritual life. The second result was a movement within the Church of Scotland to free it from the domination of statute law, which in some ways seemed to hamper it and make it unresponsive to the new vitality, and which more generally made the Church of Scotland part of an established order in politics and society which was being challenged on all sides. The evangelicals of this period were not primarily ecclesiastical politicians, as many earlier seceders had been, but they were driven to ecclesiastical politics because the existing system frustrated them in their higher aims. Purely ecclesiastical affairs were at that time so inextricably intermingled with matters which would now be regarded as civil, partly because of the responsibility of the church for poor relief and education, that the changes in the parochial system which were necessary for the extension and intensification of the church's work could not be made by the church on its own authority. The Assembly, under the sway of the evangelicals, passed acts which in effect defied statute law, and case after case arose in which the law courts inevitably interpreted the Assembly's actions as illegal. The church was not its own master. The consequence of the recurrent conflict was the decision of the more determined evangelicals to withdraw from the state connection, and in the 'Disruption' of 1843 about thirty-nine per cent of the ministers of the establishment, followed by about a third of the people, left it, to form the Free Church of Scotland.

Until less than a generation ago, the various secessions, including the Disruption, explained the existence of churches which together outnumbered the establishment. Now they explain only the existence of a few very minor presbyterian denominations. But they should not be forgotten. It is useful to recall that the Church of Scotland of today includes bodies which in the eighteenth century were excommunicating each other, and which much more recently regarded union between them as inconceivable. And it is hard to avoid the conclusion that the secessions disclosed a weakness in the conception of the church. The best defence of the secessions is that unity was subordinated to truth, but truth was too often found in some theoretical scruple or some minor point of controversy. It was demonstrated, too, that the presbyterian system to some extent facilitated schism, for any handful of disgruntled ministers could constitute themselves a presbytery and start a new 'church'.

At the same time, while it is easy to sneer at the divisive tendencies of Scottish presbyterianism, and to think it almost comic that the presbyterian body should divide and subdivide until there were about eight sections, most of them claiming to be the true church of Scotland, yet there was a certain nobility about it, not least in the great Disruption, when, as it was said, stipends worth £100,000 were signed away and so many ministers left their comfortable manses to 'cast themselves on such provision as God in his providence may afford'.

With the Disruption, not only was Scottish society split, from the peerage downwards, but so many ministers had seceded and so many congregations had divided that there was a duplication of the entire ecclesiastical organisation, and also of the educational system, in schools and in training colleges for teachers and ministers. The Free Church had many wealthy and influential supporters, and the generosity and enthusiasm of its people made it possible to erect churches and schools and to maintain ministers and teachers throughout the length and breadth of the land. There may have been some truth in the gibe that if the 'Free Kirk' was 'the wee kirk, the kirk without the steeple', the 'Auld Kirk' was 'the cauld kirk, the kirk without the people', but in fact the material achievements of the Free Church were conspicuous; it is a striking commentary on this that in Edinburgh today the General Assembly of the reunited Church of Scotland meets in the former Assembly Hall of the Free Church, the former Free Church College houses the University Faculty of Divinity, and it is the former Free Church Training College for Teachers which is the one still in use. Alike in scholarship, in material resources and in spiritual worth the Free Church was the rival, and more than the rival, of the establishment.

Except for the Disruption, the whole tendency since 1820, when the two sections of New Light Seceders set the example, has been towards reunion within the presbyterian body. The complicated processes involved need not be recounted, and it may suffice to explain the situation as it had taken shape just before 1900. The Free Church had attracted into its fold the majority of the United Original Secession Church (formed in 1842 from two groups of Old Light Seceders) and in 1876 the majority of the Reformed Presbyterians. The United Presbyterian Church, which had been formed in 1847 from a union of the Relief Church with the United Secession Church (itself a union of most of the New Light Seceders) was the other large dissenting presbyterian body. There were three small denominations—the minorities of United Original Seceders and Reformed Presbyterians who had declined to enter into unions, and the Free Presbyterians, who left the Free Church in 1893 because they found its theological standards too liberal.

The United Presbyterian Church inherited from the Relief Church the 'voluntary' principle, which had also been accepted by the New Light Seceders. The Free Church, on the other hand, stood for the principle of establishment, but was in practice the most striking object lesson in what could be achieved on a voluntary basis. And the lesson became more pointed when, in 1900, the majority of the Free Church —having renounced their belief in the duty of the civil power to maintain the church—joined with the United Presbyterian Church to form the United Free Church. This was not only a demonstration that a voluntary body could reach a position of the first importance—for the united church had 1700 ministers, as against 1400 in the Church of Scotland—but it meant that should negotiations be opened with the establishment the United Free Church would not be a humble suppliant seeking admission, but a powerful negotiator able to demand substantial concessions as the price of union.

Some of the obstacles which had stood in the way of union between the Free Church and the establishment had been removed shortly after the Disruption, and in 1874 patronage was abolished. Negotiations for union began in 1909 and, after interruption by the First World War, were completed in 1929. Two very important changes were made in the political and financial position of the Church of Scotland before the United Free Church could join it. In 1921 Parliament approved certain Declaratory Articles in which the Church of Scotland asserted its 'right and power, subject to no civil authority, to legislate, and to adjudicate finally, in all matters of doctrine, worship, government and discipline'. This acknowledgement looks like a belated concession of Andrew Melville's demands, and would seem to have secured ecclesiastical independence as far as it can be secured in a country where there is no written constitution and where Parliament is technically omnicompetent, but the question has been raised whether the Church of Scotland's power to determine its own doctrine, worship, discipline and government is complete as long as the sovereign takes an oath to maintain it as it was in 1707 and whether, therefore, the Church can legally abolish synods or revive the office of bishop. In 1925 the Church of Scotland (Property and Endowments) Act dealt with finance. Since the comprehensive settlement of ecclesiastical revenues made by Charles I, the ministers of the parishes had been maintained from the teinds (tithes) or dues paid in lieu thereof, which fluctuated according to the value of grain, and the proprietors of land in each parish had been obliged to build and maintain churches and manses. In 1925 the income from teinds was in effect 'frozen' at its existing level, payment towards stipends became a charge on the land, fixed in perpetuity, and the 'heritors' were relieved of their obligations in the erection and maintenance of buildings. The endowments so retained were valued at about £300,000 annually. Two minor changes were also made, affecting the General Assembly; after 1926 the Lord High Commissioner, the sovereign's representative at the Assembly, ceased to claim the right (abandoned in practice long before) to appoint the date and place of the next meeting; and in 1929 the burgh representatives—the last vestige of the three estates—disappeared from the Assembly. It is plain that, so far from the Free Church and the United Presbyterian Church having compromised their principles by entering into union with the Church of Scotland, it was the latter which had conceded almost everything for which the Seceders and the founders of the Free Church had contended.

The process of reunion within the presbyterian bodies went one stage further in 1956, when the remnant of the United Original Secession Church wound up its affairs and was absorbed in the establishment.

The example which that minority set has not yet been followed by the other remnants which survive from earlier unions—the Reformed Presbyterians, the Free Church and the United Free Church—or by the Free Presbyterians. These bodies are all small, the first of them very small indeed, and the Free Church and Free Presbyterian Church are strongest in the Highlands. The United Free Church, which was presented with a great challenge when it resolved to 'continue' in 1929, has shown considerable vitality and readiness to experiment, for it assigns an especially important place to the elders, who can be moderators of presbyteries, it was the first Presbyterian church in Europe to open all offices, including the ministry, to women, and it is inclined to affiliations with Congregationalism. The others are strongly conservative, severed from the main tendencies in the national life of the present time and always ready with forthright denunciations of their more liberal contemporaries and of current decadence in morals and politics. There is this to be said for the minorities, that they have adhered firmly to their principles, while the majorities which entered into unions were sometimes swayed by considerations which led them to deviate from their original strictness. That a minority could have not merely principle and logic on its side, but also law, was demonstrated in the famous Free Church case following on the union of 1900, when the highest court in Britain decided that the non-union minority, the continuing Free Church or 'Wee Frees', had adhered to Free Church principles while the majority had abandoned them, and was therefore entitled to the property of the Free Church.

It is these successive unions, and especially the two great unions of 1900 and 1919, which gave the Church of Scotland its preponderance in Scotland today. It is not quite true to say, as is often said, that the Church of Scotland has retained the allegiance of the people of Scotland much more effectively than the Church of England has retained that of the people of England. The Church of Scotland, it is true, has recovered lost ground and has completely transformed its position from what it was before 1900, when it was only one presbyterian church among many. But it may be said that the Church of Scotland has made the best of both worlds and has in the end benefited from the zeal engendered by the intensive ecclesiastical rivalries of the nineteenth century as well as by the enormous effort, spiritual and intellectual, which went into the making of the unions.

A church so formed contains heterogeneous elements representing very diverse traditions, and it can be said right away that it would not long retain its unity but for the fact that the twentieth-century notions of rigidity and uniformity are much less exacting than were those of earlier times.

9

THE NON-PRESBYTERIAN CHURCHES

THE Scottish Episcopalians, the product of the schism of 1690, though they did not have secessions on the presbyterian model, were disunited in the eighteenth century. Many of the clergy and people took advantage of the Act of Toleration of 1712, whereby Episcopalians who were prepared to accept the parliamentary settlement of the succession (ultimately on the house of Hanover) were given protection in worshipping according to the 'liturgy of the Church of England'. Thus originated the 'qualified' congregations. As they used the English Prayer Book, were attended by English immigrants to Scotland, and (because the Scottish bishops were all Jacobites) had to draw their clergy from England, they were known also as 'English' congregations. They increased in strength, especially in the Lowland towns, in the second half of the eighteenth century, when Jacobitism had become obviously a dying cause, and by 1800 they were numerous and influential.

The history of the Jacobite, or 'non-juring', section of the church, which refused to accept the Hanoverian kings, is more picturesque, because of their zealous support of the 'Old Pretender' in the rebellion of 1715 and of the 'Young Pretender' in 1745. After the 'Fifteen it became illegal, on pain of imprisonment, for their clergy to hold services for congregations exceeding eight in number, and there were many prosecutions for violation of the law. In the 'Forty-Five, ten episcopalian presbyters were among the prisoners, and one of them, although a chaplain who had never borne arms, was executed. After this rising, many episcopalian chapels were burned down, the number for whom services could be conducted was reduced to four, penalties were imposed on the laity, and, with an act making it impossible for any presbyter in Scottish orders to qualify for toleration, a deliberate attempt was made to extinguish this native branch of the Episcopal Church. These severe statutes, although not consistently applied, resulted in a great decline in the strength of the non-jurors, who, however, retained the support of the 'generality of the people' in parts of the north-eastern counties and of the West Highlands, and of many lairds elsewhere. Today there are some forty or fifty congregations which can trace their continuous history, through the days of persecution, back to the time when episcopacy was the order of the established Church of Scotland. When the church was at the lowest ebb of its fortunes, it was the instrument of the transmission of the episcopal succession to the American Church. After the American colonies became independent in 1783, the English bishops, in an established church, could not consecrate Americans who were no longer subjects of King George, and Samuel Seabury then applied for consecration to the 'pious and venerable bishops' of Scotland, who 'in the school of adversity had learned to renounce the pomps and grandeur of the world' and who conferred on the American 'a free, valid and purely ecclesiastical episcopacy'.

In the intervals between persecution, when the non-jurors had freedom to wrangle, they had proved themselves almost as quarrelsome as their presbyterian contemporaries. They differed over the machinery of administration and over the method of appointing bishops, and also over liturgical matters. When the Episcopalians began their separate existence at the revolution, their worship had been barely distinguishable from that of the Presbyterians, but in the early years of the eighteenth century there had been a liturgical revival. While the 'qualified' congregations were of course tied to 'the liturgy of the Church of England', the non-jurors turned to the

Communion Office of the Scottish Prayer Book of 1637, which was modified by successive revisions until in 1764 it reached a form not radically different from that in use today. There was, in the course of this development, a good deal of controversy about certain 'usages' like the mixed chalice, reservation and the use of consecrated oil in confirmation.

With the death in 1788 of Charles Edward Stewart, the 'Young Pretender', for whom the non-jurors had prayed as 'Charles III', they decided to accept King George, and four years later an Act of Parliament legalized the ministry of Scottish Episcopalian presbyters on certain conditions, including of course prayer for the royal family by name. There was now no obstacle to union between the 'qualified' congregations and the erstwhile non-jurors, and in the early nineteenth century most of the former agreed to accept the jurisdiction of the Scottish bishops.

Nineteenth-century developments went far to transform the Episcopal Church, until in externals it is hardly recognizable as an heir of the church established before 1690. Partly in consequence of the union of the non-juring and 'qualified' sections, there was a movement towards conformity with England. The Thirty-Nine Articles of the Church of England were imposed by the act of 1792 and were accepted as a doctrinal standard in 1804, the Prayer Book became compulsory for Morning and Evening Prayer (1828), the surplice was first recommended (1811) and later enjoined (1838). The English term 'rector' displaced the Scots 'parson', the English 'priest' displaced the Scots 'presbyter', the English 'vestry' was introduced to designate the board of managers of a congregation (and the kirk session of elders, which Episcopalians had retained in the eighteenth century, was discarded). Episcopalians resent their church being called the 'English church', but efforts seem constantly to be made to efface the evidence of its Scottish pedigree. For a time even the Scottish Communion Office was depressed in favour of the English, but more recently (1929) a Scottish Book of Common Prayer has been authorized. The movement towards conformity with England had the result that by statutes passed in 1840 and 1864 Scottish Episcopalian orders received full recognition in England. The fact that this recognition was not given until so comparatively recently is an effective answer to the charge that the Episcopal Church is an offshoot of the Church of England. As the concept of an 'Anglican Communion' developed, the Scottish Episcopal Church took its place within it, in much the same way as the Church of Scotland was associated with the Presbyterian Alliance, but there was never any question of submitting to English jurisdiction. During the time of persecution the allocation of districts to bishops had been somewhat haphazard, but ultimately the fourteen old dioceses were allotted among seven bishops. The office of archbishop was allowed to lapse early in the eighteenth century, and instead recourse was had to the ancient office of 'Primus'.

A second conspicuous feature of the nineteenth and early twentieth centuries, the result of the influence of the Oxford or Tractarian Movement, was the introduction of 'ornaments', vestments and ritual previously unknown, for hitherto the Scottish Episcopalians, although 'high' in their sacramental doctrine, had been 'low' in their practice. This movement caused a minor schism, with the formation of a fresh crop of 'English' congregations, and this schism is not yet quite extinct. It also resulted in considerable diversity in usage, which still exists.

Neither conformity with England nor the ritualistic development did much to commend the Episcopal Church to the Scots, and whereas in the nineteenth century it received a considerable accession of strength from Presbyterians who preferred its modest ritual to the bleak services of their own denominations, in more recent times Presbyterians have been able to find dignity and beauty in worship in the Church of Scotland, while the Episcopal Church has suffered losses through the alienation of congregations by innovating clergy.

The Roman Catholic Church, except in so far as its mere existence led to the recurrence of occasional 'popish scares' (all the more inflammatory because it was mysterious and inconspicuous), played only a minor part in Scottish life until quite recently. In the late sixteenth and early seventeenth centuries, while there was in certain regions what has been called 'a Catholic "interest", politically conservative, allergic to the ethos of the New Religion but in the last resort singularly indeterminate',[1] active Romanism was almost extinct, for there were hardly any priests except a few chaplains to private families, and they made no widespread impact. Spasmodic missionary work was done in some western districts from time to time, but continuous and sustained effort began only in the 1690s. At that point, as the new presbyterian establishment was hopelessly undermanned, with no footing in the north and west, and the Episcopalians were a divided and bewildered body without the resources to maintain their hold in Highland areas, a kind of vacuum existed, of which Roman Catholic missionaries took advantage. The continuous history of the Roman Catholic Church in Scotland, as an organized institution, dates substantially from that period. Most of the areas now regarded as the homes of indigenous Romanism were in fact converted at the end of the seventeenth century, and had been Protestant a generation earlier.

Even with the work done at this time, the total of Romanists in the country would seem to have been only between 20,000 and 30,000 throughout the eighteenth century. Then in a hundred years came a twentyfold increase. It was due almost wholly to the great immigration from Ireland in the nineteenth century, to the high birth-rate among the immigrants and to the insistence that the children of 'mixed marriages' should be brought up as Roman Catholics. There have been accessions of other immigrants—Italians and Poles —but right down to the present day no observer can fail to be impressed by the approximation of the Roman Catholic population to the population of Irish descent. Over the whole country the nominal Roman Catholic strength is about fifteen per cent of the population, but in the Glasgow region the proportion of children who attend Roman Catholic schools

[1] David Mathew, *Scotland under Charles I*, 1955, p. 20.

is over forty per cent. In many parts of the country this church does not even now have much importance in the life of the community, partly because of its racial character, which helps to keep it apart and tends to antagonize native Scots, and partly because its members were largely drawn from the lowest social classes. It was not until 1878 that Roman Catholic bishops were appointed to Scottish territorial titles.

One source of strength of the Roman Catholic Church, from the national point of view, lies in its claim to be the representative of the medieval church. The situation is vastly different in England, where the material evidence of the continuity of the Church of England is plain for all to see. In any rural parish in England, and in many a town parish, one may find a long list of incumbents, going back without a break perhaps as far as the Norman Conquest; every see has its continuous list of bishops; the historic buildings are in the hands of the Church of England. In Scotland, while such medieval buildings as remain in use for worship are mostly in the hands of the Church of Scotland, the Roman Catholic Church can make almost as good a case for continuity as the Church of Scotland or the Episcopal Church. In popular usage, the Middle Ages are 'Roman Catholic times', and the Scots were all 'Roman Catholics' until John Knox came on the scene. This has the disadvantage, however, of identifying the modern Roman Catholic Church with medieval corruptions and of ignoring the changes which adapted it to new conditions—and kept it one step ahead of even its most determined Anglican imitators.

The Roman Catholics have taken full advantage of the educational provisions which compel local authorities to maintain schools for their children. It is true that these provisions applied to all denominational schools, but whereas the schools of the Episcopal Church, which in the nineteenth century were a valuable sphere of missionary work, not least in the poorer areas of the cities, have almost all been closed, the Romans have suceeded in making the authorities carry out their obligations, and there are also separate training colleges for teachers. This fact is in some ways a great source of strength, but it does help to segregate the Roman Catholics from the general population, it has been known to arouse animosity among ratepayers, and it renews the Protestant suspicion that if the Romans were confident of the truth of their teaching they would be less sensitive about the risk of exposing their children to non-denominational instruction.

Among the other non-presbyterian denominations, the largest and the one with the strongest indigenous character is the Congregational Church. The 'Old Scotch Independents' dated from 1768, and in the late 1790s there arose many independent evangelical congregations which were formed into the Congregational Union in 1857. In the 1840s James Morison left the United Secession Church and with other like-minded ministers formed the Evangelical Union (Morisonians). In 1896 these two bodies amalgamated as the Congregational Union of Scotland, but in true Scottish fashion some churches remained outside the union. The congregationalist proportion of the population—about two per cent —is approximately the same as the episcopalian. Baptist churches in Scotland date from 1750, but they were not numerous, and their separatist tendencies kept them apart until 1869, when most of them joined in the Baptist Union. Methodism is perhaps the most purely English of all the non-presbyterian denominations. John Wesley paid no less than twenty-two visits to Scotland, the last of them in 1790, and while his chief influence was in the encouragement of evangelical tendencies generally, inside as well as outside the establishment, several chapels for his followers were opened in his own day. The strength of Methodism was to lie mainly in the cities, but like other denominations with an evangelical approach it attracted a good deal of support in rural areas where the established church was comparatively inactive, notably in Shetland. Baptists and Methodists together account for no more than one and a half per cent of the population.

10

INTER-CHURCH RELATIONS

THE majority of Scottish churchmen belong to an 'established' church. Since the changes made in the 1920s, the meaning of establishment has so altered that it might now be more accurate to speak of an 'official and endowed' church, but the concept of 'establishment' is warmly cherished by Scottish Presbyterians. For this there are historical reasons. It has been said, a little harshly, that in England establishment is a natural growth, while in Scotland it was a parliamentary status conferred as a political reward. This is true in the narrow sense that one cannot point to an English enactment comparable to the statute of 1690 on which the present Scottish establishment is based. But it is true in a more profound sense. In England an episcopal system has been acknowledged by the law as far back as legal memory extends, it existed for centuries before any other was thought of, and no other has ever been legally established. But in Scotland the presbyterian system was a novelty which required authorization by statute, it was more than once disestablished, and in the past the Church of Scotland relied on establishment to distinguish it not only from the Episcopal Church but also from other presbyterian churches of comparable importance. It is not hard to understand why the Church of Scotland is so insistent that it is the church 'by law established'.

Indeed, reviewing Scottish history from the Reformation, it is a little difficult to avoid the conclusion that the principal mark of 'the Church of Scotland' is establishment. Few Presbyterians have ever seriously contested the claim of the church of episcopalian constitution which existed in the seventeenth century to be 'the Church of Scotland'—an admission hard to reconcile with the claim that presbytery is *jure divino*. The Presbyterians at no time formed 'the Church of Scotland' unless they had statutory recognition. Equally, the Episcopalians ceased to constitute 'the Church of Scotland' when they lost parliamentary recognition, for the presbyterian view was that ordinations by bishops were valid as long as the bishops had statutory authority, but that after the bishops were 'deprived' by Parliament in 1689 their ordinations ceased to be valid.

If 'establishment' is one mark of the church, the second is that it is 'the national church'. Not only does this concept emphasize that it is the church of the majority of Scottish churchmen today and that it is, as it claims to be, in historical continuity with the church of earlier times, but when a Scot insists that his church shall be what he calls 'the national church'—when he rejects the Roman Catholic Church because it is largely alien in personnel and because it is run from Rome and when he rejects the Episcopal Church because he ignorantly supposes that it is run from Canterbury—he is in a long and not dishonourable tradition. His nation is one which, through centuries of adversity, preserved its political independence, and he cherishes the distinctive national characteristics and institutions which still survive. The Scot often feels, not entirely without justification, that England, although she lost the war, has been altogether too successful in winning the peace, and that although she failed to conquer Scotland in a military sense she subverts Scottish nationality in the cultural and economic spheres and would willingly do the same in the ecclesiastical. In view of Scottish history, it seems unlikely that any church will secure the allegiance of the majority of the Scottish people unless it can advance some pretensions to be considered 'the national church'.

It was no human design which determined the pattern of the reunions of the nineteenth and twentieth centuries, but it was undoubtedly logical that they should precede any serious attempt to come to terms with the Episcopalians. Yet the presbyterian reunions have not rendered the way easier to an understanding between Anglicans and the Church of Scotland. Until 1900, when there were still three separate major presbyterian denominations, the Episcopal Church in Scotland, although smaller than any of the three, was comparable to them: in those days the Edinburgh Post Office Directory, for example, devoted approximately a page apiece to the Church of Scotland, the United Presbyterians, the Free Church and the Episcopal Church. The pattern of reunions could not then have been forecast. And after 1900, when the United Free Church was formed, there was still a chance that the Church of Scotland would prefer union with the Episcopalians rather than capitulation to its great presbyterian competitor, and the prospects of an Anglican understanding with the Church of Scotland were almost as promising in the early years of this century as they have ever been. With the opening of discussions with the United Free Church, however, the Church of Scotland began to face another way, and with the union of 1929 the reunited church comprehended—it might be too much to say that it absorbed—elements which were more hostile to Anglicanism than the 'Auld Kirk' had been. The unions of 1900 and 1929 also had the effect of making the proportionate numerical strength of the Scottish Episcopal Church almost negligible, though it retained peculiar significance in that an accommodation with it would give the Church of Scotland a new relationship with the world-wide Anglican Communion.

Recent negotiations for closer presbyterian-episcopalian understanding must be viewed in the light of the fact that in many ways the two churches, or elements within them, have been growing much closer in their beliefs and practices, and some of the old obstacles have been eliminated.

Both churches have departed from strict enforcement of their confessional standards. All that is asked of an ordinand in the Church of Scotland is that he should accept 'the fundamental doctrines of the Christian faith' contained in the standards, and in the Episcopal Church all that is required of a

H

presbyter is that he should declare his 'assent' to the Thirty-Nine Articles. It may be doubted if a united church would display any more diversity in theology than the Church of Scotland and the Episcopal Church individually do at present. If, on one side, some Episcopalians hold a theology of the Sacraments not to be found in the Church of Scotland, it is equally true that the latter accommodated a strong element of modernism which is hardly to be found in the Episcopal Church (where the liturgy has done much to ensure that central doctrines like the Incarnation and the Atonement continue to be proclaimed in traditional dogmatic language). But, while diversity exists, reunion discussions have disclosed that in the present state of theological opinion there is a greater degree of unity than was previously thought possible, and very large areas of theology have never had to be brought into question at all.

The Presbyterians have abandoned the exclusive claim of a divine right for their system, and no longer deny that other systems as well are agreeable to the Word of God. To that extent, Presbyterians are no longer contending for something which they believe to be indispensable. A comparable liberalism has led them to modify their attitude to admission to Communion. For generations they guarded their Communion tables and their fonts with a severity quite unknown to Anglicans; no one was admitted to Communion without being approved as to his faith and morals, and certainly no 'prelatist' would have been admitted (except in the Relief Church, where a more liberal view prevailed). In recent years, however, the Church of Scotland has ceased to inspect the credentials of those who come to its tables. This is a revolutionary change from the days when it was reckoned an offence for a minister to issue a 'promiscuous invitation to the Lord's table',[1] and when unmarried mothers, repelled by presbyterian discipline, brought their infants for baptism in the more kindly Episcopal Church—'the kirk,' as one of them said, 'where they baptize a' the bairns'.

[1] *Fasti Ecclesiae Scoticanae, III*, 349.

Some Presbyterians are much less confident than they once were that there is nothing to be said for a system of oversight by individuals rather than by committees, and there have from time to time been proposals for the revival of 'superintendents'. As far back as 1932 a leading presbyterian divine described the revival of a modified episcopate as 'not a remote contingency'.[1] A good deal of discussion at this level is now somewhat unrealistic, because in an organization as big as the Church of Scotland a great deal of the real power has fallen into the hands of permanent officials—ecclesiastical bureaucrats—who may conceivably exercise the functions of superintendents, or even bishops, without being specially set apart for the task. The spiritual and disciplinary functions of the elders, whether acting corporately as a kirk session, or individually as pastors of districts, have for the most part been quietly laid aside, though some efforts have been made at their revival. Apart from assisting in the distribution of the elements at Communion—which he does only by use and wont—the elder is often not much more than a member of a congregational board of management. He may visit a section of the congregation and distribute Communion cards, but it is not unknown for laymen to do this in the Episcopal Church. There is still disagreement among the Presbyterians as to the precise significance of the eldership, for some hold that the elder is 'ordained', and equate 'elder' with 'minister'—and indeed with 'bishop'—while others regard the elder, in spite of his appointment for life, as still a layman who has merely been 'admitted' to his office.

On the episcopalian side, some developments have been contrary to the liberalism prevailing in the Church of Scotland, and equally a departure from earlier traditions. Confirmation, disregarded in seventeenth-century Scotland, and in England so neglected that in the eighteenth century it was possible to reach the episcopal bench without having been confirmed, was emphasized firstly by non-jurors and then by the Tractarians, and became a prerequisite to admission to Holy

[1] Charles L. Warr, 'The Scottish Church' in *A Scotsman's Heritage*.

Communion. Likewise, from the time of the non-jurors the concept of the exclusive validity of episcopalian ordinations made headway, despite the fact that the episcopal system had been reintroduced to Scotland under a scheme of compromise which involved the recognition of presbyterian orders. On the other hand, however, the tendency has been towards the extension of the responsibility of the laity. Congregational business is managed by an elected vestry, which commonly has a voice in the appointment of the incumbent. In the Representative Church Council (established in 1876) and the Diocesan Councils, lay men and women are present, approximately equal in numbers with the clergy, to manage the church's finances, and this task, in a church largely dependent on funds collected year by year from its members, means the oversight of most aspects of the church's work. Presbyterians need to be reminded that a Diocesan Council, besides reviewing most church activities, each year decides what salary is to be paid to the bishop. From 1905 the laity, as members of the Consultative Council on Church Legislation, expressed their views on the canons, the liturgy and other matters which in the long run involve doctrine, and in 1963 the Provincial Synod was reconstituted, with lay as well as clerical members, to deal with those subjects. In the election of bishops, the Episcopal Church has gone back (since 1863) to the primitive model of election by the clergy and laity of the diocese, and in such an electoral body the laymen very often find themselves in a majority. In short, most of the church's affairs are conducted by councils, boards and committees in which bishops have no special powers and in which the vote of any lay person is of equal value to that of a bishop. And in according to lay women a position of complete equality with laymen, in every function save electing bishops, the Episcopal Church was ahead of the Church of Scotland.

Presbyterians are apt to be resentful when it is suggested that their church does not make provision for the representation of the laity and that the practice of appointing elders for life excludes the laity from any part in church affairs. But that the Church of Scotland is in a real sense more clerical than the Episcopal Church, and that it is less ready to turn to the laity for service, must be the conclusion of anyone familiar with the less clerical atmosphere of the Episcopal Church. Because of the very absence of the eldership, the Episcopal Church calls on the services of any layman, without conferring on him any 'ordination'—unless his confirmation be so regarded —for a wide range of service, indeed for everything save administration of the Sacraments (and laymen are now quite commonly authorized to administer the chalice). If there is some substance in the presbyterian charge that the Episcopal Church interposes a needless barrier, in confirmation, between the layman and Communion, it is equally true that the Presbyterians interpose a needless barrier, in ordination to the eldership, between the layman and participation in church affairs.

The developments in worship in both churches in the last hundred years have been manifold, but the most profound of them have arisen from a renewed emphasis on the Holy Communion, though each church has expressed the emphasis in a different way. In the Episcopal Church the great achievement was the recovery of the weekly Communion. At first the all but universal practice was a celebration every Sunday at an early hour, with a late celebration only once a month or on great festivals, while mattins retained its place as the chief service. More 'advanced' churches then went in for a late Choral Eucharist, a celebration at which few of the congregation communicated. More recently there has been a new fashion. The early said celebration and the late choral celebration are alike being laid aside in favour of a Communion, usually sung, at an hour like 9, 9.30 or 10—a celebration at which all present normally communicate. This service is an approach to the ideal of the Reformers.

In the Church of Scotland the renewed emphasis on Communion has been expressed in a different way. There may here and there be a weekly celebration, but in general it is true that celebrations remain infrequent and that when they take place they are still great corporate, congregational occasions. The infrequent celebration, however, stands alongside the restoration of a genuine and unmistakable Ante-Communion as the normal Sunday morning service. Thus, although Episcopalians deserve credit for their success in going some way to overcome the medieval prejudice against frequent Communion, the Presbyterians on their side have never lost the ideal of a corporate, a congregational, action.

Not only has there thus come to be a great measure of agreement on the principles underlying worship, but even in externals there have been changes which have brought conformity nearer. In the Church of Scotland the essentially auditory churches of the eighteenth and early nineteenth centuries, often designed on a T-plan with three arms converging on a pulpit set in the middle of the longest wall, and sometimes as single-chamber buildings with a massive pulpit at one end, were modified in the late nineteenth century by the introduction of enormous organ cases which covered one end of the church with an overpowering array of organ pipes against which the pulpit was set. The earlier design had allowed for the existence, either permanently or temporarily, of long tables around which the communicants could assemble, but the modification brought a small Communion Table placed inconspicuously in front of the pulpit and often a mere incidental on a platform dedicated primarily to the accommodation of a choir. In every new building of recent years, and in most reconstructions, the pulpit has been removed to one side, the organ pipes banished to a less conspicuous position and the chancel occupied by a seemly table which is unmistakably the focus of worship. All of the service except the sermon may be conducted from the Table, and the increased respect for the church building and the sanctity which it represents is reflected in the growing habit of having baptisms and marriages in church, whereas a century ago this was (contrary to the principles of the reformers) all but unknown. On the other hand, the practice of distributing the Communion to the congregation in their pews, which came in with the abandonment of the long tables, remains usual.

The 'praise' of Presbyterians had for long been strictly scriptural, and originally confined to the metrical psalms, to which were added in the eighteenth century metrical paraphrases of other passages of Scripture. In the nineteenth century, hymn books were introduced. The current *Church Hymnary* contains a range of devotional pieces as rich as that in Anglican collections, and it includes also those 'forms'— the Lord's Prayer, the Creeds, the Gloria and Canticles— which were discarded in the 1640s. Prose psalms are sometimes sung, but it is hard to convince presbyterian congregations that they are capable of singing anything which is not in metre and rhyme, and the Authorized Version, used by the Church of Scotland, does not seem to lend itself so well to singing as the Prayer Book Version. Liturgies were introduced experimentally from the middle of last century, and there is at present an authorized Book of Common Order (though its use is optional). It was formerly the practice of Presbyterians to sit for praise and stand for prayer, but it is nowadays usual to reverse these postures, though kneeling for prayer is not unknown. (Some of the smaller presbyterian bodies still use only the psalms, reject instrumental music and adhere to the old postures.)

In their general design and furnishings, episcopalian churches differ little from the latest presbyterian models, except that more of them have choir stalls on both sides of the chancel. Again, while Presbyterians have gone a long way with stained glass and statues, frontals changing with the liturgical seasons and coloured cassocks for choirs, episcopalian churches are in the main more decorative in their ornaments and vesture. However, there is such a wide variety in both churches that it might not be difficult to maintain that some presbyterian churches are 'higher' than the 'lowest' of the episcopalian churches. While the Holy Table recovered its dominant position earlier among the Episcopalians than among the Presbyterians, the recent Anglican experiments in moving it forward from the east wall and celebrating from behind it, facing the people, offer a new prospect of assimilation of the two churches.

All those indications of the tendency of the two churches to approximate are an important part of the background to the official conversations which have been going on intermittently for more than a generation. As soon as the Church of Scotland had achieved its union with the United Free Church in 1929 it began to look towards a wider union. It was in 1932 that it first engaged in talks with Anglicans, and since then five rounds of discussions have taken place. It might be a mistake to regard the readiness of the Church of Scotland to participate in these successive conversations as a proof of its desire for union, because it has been said that what it wants is not so much union with the Anglicans as recognition by them. The first and second rounds of talks (1932–4 and 1949–1951) were between the Church of Scotland and the Church of England, presumably because the Scots, preening themselves on their status as a 'national' and 'established' church, declined to negotiate except with another 'national' and 'established' church. Representatives of the Scottish Episcopal Church and the Presbyterian Church of England were present at those negotiations only as observers. This arrangement meant that little attention was paid to the Scottish Episcopal Church, which differed from the Church of England in offering a native, and not an alien, episcopate and in possessing an episcopacy free from all taint of 'prelacy', and which was proud of the free and independent status it had acquired at the cost of disendowment and disestablishment. It also meant that the talks were insufficiently related to the approximation which had already taken place in Scotland between the Church of Scotland and the Scottish Episcopal Church.

When the third round of talks started, in 1953, the two non-established churches were full participants and the report from this round, presented in 1957, went much further than the two earlier reports, which had been concerned mainly with the enunciation of general principles about agreement on certain essential doctrines and with recommendations for intercommunion and exchange of preachers. This time, in 1957, an actual plan for union was proposed, along the lines of a mutual adaptation of the two systems in their order and ministry through the introduction of 'bishops-in-presbytery' to the Church of Scotland and officers akin to elders to the Church of England. Such a concept did not seem to represent a drastic step to anyone who knows Scottish history. The hostility which the proposal encountered in Scotland arose partly from two causes. Nothing had been done to prepare the ground— a fact which itself gave rise to allegations of secrecy and plotting—and some sections of the press, from which almost everyone derived his acquaintance with the proposal, were violently, often hysterically, hostile. Secondly, far too many Scots who were not active churchmen at all became extremely vocal, on a matter which was not their business, with unreasonable and unreasoning condemnation. One of the stories which went around was that one vocal critic of the scheme, when reminded that he had always professed himself an atheist, replied, 'Yes, but I'm a Presbyterian atheist.' Whether a shallow nationalism was the main element in the opposition has been debated, but it was noticeable that some of those who were most abusive of bishops were among those whose national pride made them most eager that the Church of Scotland should be represented in the House of Lords, a proposal which was as much at variance with presbyterian theories as is the 'bishop-in-presbytery'.

In 1959 the General Assembly, by a small majority, declared the proposals of the Report unacceptable. Thus, at a time when much thought was being given to the theory and practice of church order, and when other churches were earnestly and critically examining their ministries, the Church of Scotland decided against change. The decision seemed to ignore the many schemes of reunion under consideration throughout the world, all of which envisaged an episcopate in any church comprehending Anglicans and Presbyterians. Yet the Assembly's decision might almost be called characteristic, in that it reflects so much of Scotland's history: it is nothing new for Scottish church life to be at variance with the trends prevailing generally throughout Christendom, it is nothing new for the Scots to consider themselves a peculiar people who have received something akin to a special revelation; and the influence of national conceit emerged in the decision of that same assembly of 1959 to rescind the act which had hitherto made it impossible for ministers of the Church of Scotland to sit alongside English bishops in the House of Lords. Yet it will remain a fact of history that the men who signed the Report of 1957 on behalf of the Church of Scotland achieved this: the Church of Scotland was brought, for the first time since 1690, seriously to consider the revival of the office of bishop.

The fourth round of conversations (1962–6) was again on a four-church basis, and produced a very thoughtful and profound, if somewhat inconclusive, report. In the course of this round the idea of direct discussions between the two Scottish churches emerged, and the next stage was to initiate formal conversations between them. From those conversations there came in 1971 another realistic plan, that the Scottish Episcopal Church should be incorporated in the Church of Scotland as a non-territorial synod, but this was thrown out by the Episcopal Church by a very small majority. Many have been disappointed, but failure to find a means of uniting a presbyterian and an episcopal church was hardly surprising in view of the fact that the Church of Scotland had meanwhile rejected a plan for union with the Congregational Church and seems no nearer than before to union with even the other presbyterian bodies in Scotland.

While the formal negotiations have thus so far not produced an acceptable plan of union, changes have been taking place, sometimes officially and sometimes unobtrusively, which have transformed the relations of the two churches. The admission of presbyterian ministers to the pulpits of the Episcopal Church, at which many Episcopalians held up their hands in horror twenty years ago, has become commonplace, joint services and even joint Communions are not rare, in some places the two denominations are sharing buildings as well as activities, and arrangements are in operation for the presence of representatives of each church on the councils, courts and boards of the other. Many see these developments, and general co-operation at local level, as far more hopeful than anything that has happened in official talks. Besides, alongside the last round of presbyterian-episcopalian conversations there have also been multi-lateral talks in which the United Free Church, the Congregationalists, the Methodists and the Churches of Christ are represented. These conversations, by bringing together the Episcopal Church and other smaller churches, open a new dimension and may be more fruitful than direct bilateral confrontation.

The Roman Catholic Church, while not engaged in any conversations designed to lead to union, has entered into discussions with both the Church of Scotland and the Episcopal Church. Perhaps among all the changes of recent years, the changes in the Roman Catholic Church have been the most far-reaching. With the authorization of a vernacular mass, the introduction of a new rite somewhat in line with the thought and practice of the reformed churches, the adoption of a central table in place of an altar and the growing part played by the laity in church affairs—and all of those supported and informed by a new impetus to Bible-reading—the Roman Catholic Church is already in a fair way to conceding what the reformers craved four centuries ago. If it also gives way to the pressure for a married clergy, makes the collegiate power of bishops a real counterpoise to the authority of the Pope, and extends the responsibility of the laity, it will be a church at which Protestants can look with a fresh eye. The Roman Church has long been a reformed church, in the sense that it has been purged of medieval abuses, but it may yet become the ultimate proof of the effectiveness of the Reformation.

FOR FURTHER READING

The best account of Scottish church history before the Reformation is A. R. McEwen, *A History of the Church in Scotland*, vol. I (Hodder and Stoughton, 1915). A shorter book is J. A. Duke, *History of the Church of Scotland to the Reformation* (Oliver and Boyd, 1937).

On the Reformation, David Hay Fleming, *The Reformation in Scotland* (Hodder and Stoughton, 1910), remains the most important work, and although the writer's point of view is ultra-Protestant his mastery of the facts is indisputable. John Knox's own *History of the Reformation* is available in an edition by W. Croft Dickinson (2 vols., Nelson, 1949). The results of recent research on the polity and worship of the reformed church will be found in Gordon Donaldson, *The Scottish Reformation* (Cambridge University Press, 1960) and *The Making of the Scottish Prayer Book of 1637* (Edinburgh University Press, 1954), and Duncan Shaw, *The General Assemblies of the Church of Scotland* (St Andrew Press, 1964).

For the whole period since the Reformation, the works of G. D. Henderson, including *The Claims of the Church of Scotland* (Hodder and Stoughton, 1951), are valuable. For the seventeenth century a stimulating guide is Rosalind Mitchison, *History of Scotland* (Methuen, 1970). W. R. Foster, *Bishop and Presbytery* (SPCK, 1958), is an important examination of the church system of the Restoration period.

For the nineteenth and early twentieth centuries, the standard work is J. R. Fleming, *The Church in Scotland, 1843–1929* (2 vols., T. and T. Clark, 1927–33). It may be supplemented by Peter F. Anson, *The Catholic Church in Modern Scotland* (Burns, Oates, 1937) and F. Goldie, *Short History of the Episcopal Church in Scotland* (SPCK, 1951).

The general survey in J. H. S. Burleigh, *A Church History of Scotland* (Oxford University Press, 1960) is comprehensive and judicious. A general account of worship is given by W. D. Maxwell, *Worship in the Church of Scotland* (Oxford University Press, 1955).

The best brief histories of Scotland are R. S. Rait, *History of Scotland* (Home University Library, 1915), and R. L. Mackie, *Short History of Scotland* (revised edition, Oliver and Boyd, 1962). Rait and G. S. Pryde, *Scotland* (2nd edn., Benn, 1954), gives a general account of Scotland to 1707, followed by a series of chapters on various aspects of the later history (including one on the churches). Documents and extracts from original sources, with commentaries, for the period to 1707, are provided in W. C. Dickinson, G. Donaldson and I. A. Milne, *A Source Book of Scottish History* (3 vols., Nelson, 1954–9), and a selection of notable documents in G. Donaldson, *Scottish Historical Documents* (Scottish Academic Press, 1970). There is no large-scale up-to-date work covering the whole of Scottish history, but volumes III and IV of the *Edinburgh History of Scotland* (Oliver and Boyd, 1965, 1968) deal with the period since 1513.

INDEX